INVISIBLE
FORCES

SCHOOL REFORM versus SCHOOL CULTURE

Julian D. Prince

A Publication of Phi Delta Kappa's
Center on Evaluation, Development, and Research
Bloomington, Indiana

Book and cover design
by
Merridee LaMantia

Library of Congress Catalogue Card Number 89-063687
ISBN 0-87367-725-0

Printed in the United States of America

CONTENTS

FOREWORD

Educators have always been squeezed by pressures to conform to social norms on the one hand and to take risks to shape a new social order on the other. How they shape the schools depends upon their response to those contradictory pressures. School culture is defined by the attitudes and behaviors of those who teach and learn there. The call for reform comes when expectations change about the outcomes of learning and teaching, and there is dissatisfaction with the way things are.

Julian Prince offers some practical ways to think about change in schools and the implications for leaders in education who must help shape the vision for change and implement an action plan that results in better learning for all students. The conceptual models, strategies for planning, decision making processes, assessment techniques, and case studies that Prince sets forth all offer hope for those who want to take action to improve schools. But it is important to approach this book with a clear understanding of the changing context in which schools operate; we must accept the notion that more of the same will not be good enough. Educators can no longer define their mission simply as providing basic literacy and numeracy for those who want to stay in school long enough to achieve them.

It is not new to acknowledge change as a constant. Without question, we will see enormous changes in American public education in the years just ahead. Unprecedented changes are taking place in our society, placing demands on the educational system that it is ill prepared to meet in its traditional form. Great numbers of students are coming to our schools with needs requiring far different approaches to learning and teaching than we have traditionally taken. And all evidence indicates that we are seeing only the beginning.

At the same time, the needs of society and its expectations for public schools are changing rapidly. Schools still have the mandate that has been reached through consensus over many years — to foster citizenship, promote literacy, produce workers, and cultivate personal self-fulfillment. However, educators must recognize that they are preparing students to enter a society of which we can see only the bare outlines, and it looks considerably different from anything we have known in the past.

To understand how profound the changes in the student population will be, one needs only to review some current demographic trends. We are told, for example, that by the year 2000 one in three of us will be non-white. Among the young, the percentage of non-whites will continue to be even greater. Early in the next century, Hispanics will outnumber African Americans to become the largest single ethnic minority in America.

Immigration will continue to be a major factor in our population growth; two-thirds of the world's immigrants now come to America.

The most rapidly growing segment of the population is people over the age of 85. By the turn of the century, about 35 million Americans will be 65 years or older. The percentage of adults with children in school will continue to decline. Increases in non-traditional family households also will continue. Less than one family in 12 now fits the traditional family pattern of a working father, homemaker mother, with two or more children.

Some economic upward mobility will continue, but gains will be offset by concurrent downward mobility. The gap separating the "haves" and "have nots" will widen, and the traditionally strong middle class will be eroded by a growing under- and upper-class. In America, one child in five now lives in poverty. The rate of poverty among the young is now nearly seven times the rate among the old. Based on current public policy, there is little evidence that this disturbing trend will be reversed.

Every day in America 40 teenage girls give birth to their third child. We have the highest illegitimate birth rate among western nations. Children having children account for 700,000 of the 3.3 million births annually. Most of these teenage mothers have poor or no prenatal care, increasing the probability of their having premature babies or babies with low body weight and poor health. These children will enter school at high risk of failure. Many will have learning difficulties and physical handicaps.

I could go on, but the point should be clear. Schools must prepare to serve more and more students from diverse cultural backgrounds whose native language is not English and who do not have anything approaching the traditional American family background. We will educate these children in the context of a growing under-class, an apparently worsening drug abuse epidemic, and very high dropout rates. And we will attempt it in the face of a growing shortage of teachers and declining resources.

The kind of a society we will be preparing these students to live in will be determined to a large degree by dramatically changing economic developments. We know that the changing national and international economies are altering the nature of work in America. We are told we are moving toward a knowledge-based service economy that will provide fewer jobs for unskilled workers and more jobs for workers with greater technical and intellectual skills. If one of our major objectives for public education is to prepare students for work and enable them to contribute to the success of our economy, then schools must carefully think through their curriculum and the nature of their instruction. All students who graduate from high school must be able to solve problems, make sensible decisions, understand the consequences of their actions, adapt to change, cope with complexity, accept ambiguity — in short, they must be able to think for a living.

It is clear that there are many approaches that can be taken to accommodate and shape educational change. Exciting and interesting reform ideas and restructuring activities are being pursued in school districts in all parts of the country. The reader will learn of several of them here. The hope is that the ambitious reform efforts of the late 1980s and early '90s will lead to systemic changes in schools. For this to occur, educators must take what they know about learning and teaching and act on that knowledge. If they do, the culture of schools will change as will their structure and organization.

All plans for changes in our schools, regardless of their nature, must have strong, effective leadership if they are to be successful. School leaders must have a vision of what the best future of education can and must be. Leaders then must be able to transform ideas into action that helps schools become places of learning that make a difference in the lives of children. Leaders must engage others in the action and enable them to help.

As advocates for children, leaders must be passionate in pushing for innovation and change. They must be willing to announce problems as a first step in inspiring others to invent solutions. Above all, they must care about what they do despite the ambiguity that is ever present in their roles. They must recognize that the power of influence can be more effective than the power of authority.

Attitudes are important for effective leadership. Intellectual curiosity, a sincere interest in what others think, eagerness to take risks, and confidence in the future are important qualities for a leader to possess. As leaders, we must continue to educate ourselves by reading broadly, debating with colleagues, and emulating mentors and role models.

This is an exciting time to be working in public education. The opportunities to make a real difference are many. Our task will be to ask questions that challenge traditional assumptions about learning, teaching, and the role of schools. The responses must be creative and bold. We cannot ignore students whom we have not served well. The achievement gap that exists between African Americans and Hispanics on the one hand and whites and Asians on the other must be closed. Students from every group must meet our high expectations.

The invisible forces of school reform and school culture must become visible. Educational leaders have a special responsibility to create the catalysts for change, but we must be willing to examine our own practice as a first step in convincing all Americans that public education and strong schools that promote effective teaching and learning are in everybody's best interest.

The careful analysis, thoughtful reflection, and practical suggestions for action proposed by this book will help inform the debate about change in our schools, leading to better education for all children.

Thomas W. Payzant

Superintendent
San Diego City Schools

PREFACE

At the end of the yellow brick road, Dorothy and her traveling companions got their wishes — the scarecrow, a brain; the tin man, a heart; the lion, courage; and Dorothy, a trip home to Kansas. After many treacherous experiences, they learned from the munificent Oz that they already possessed everything necessary to realize their dreams. They proved this on their long journey. Through hard work and cooperation, they gained new attitudes about themselves and their abilities to reach their goals. School leaders who want to travel the road to reform may be like Dorothy and her friends. While they may have the critical elements to achieve educational reform at their disposal, they don't know how to put the elements together to effect long-lasting, systemic change.

Successful educational change does not happen overnight. Change requires strong leaders with vision and effective management skills; and it requires time — often a lot of time. Change also requires common attitudes about teaching and learning among school district personnel and community members. Superintendents play a key role in the development of these common attitudes. As educational leaders, they are in a unique position to weave the disparate elements of the school district into a cohesive whole that is supported by the community. Because of their position in the school district, superintendents are uniquely situated to observe the pieces of the educational puzzle. Managing educational reform requires constant attention to the various pieces and the many relationships within the school as well as the interface between the school and the local community.

Today there are many superintendents and local school leaders who would like to make their schools better places for children to learn. This book is written for these leaders. Its suggestions are practical, not faddish. Fundamental weaknesses in our schools will not be changed exclusively through teacher empowerment, new technology, four-day school weeks, vouchers, school/industry connection, or the newest model of clinical supervision or teacher evaluation.

Good schools are found in the *attitudes* of the entire community. At the right time and place innovative ideas may be valuable. Alone, however, they do not improve the underlying nature of a weak school program. Without community desire to have good schools and consensus about how to make a strong academic program, innovative ideas are only window dressing.

And without working on *all* aspects of school change — curriculum, discipline, personnel programs, and so forth — *at the same time*, changes will not last long.

This book will give ample evidence that given the right conditions of consensus, school district initiated reform can spread across separate school sites, despite different school and community settings. This can occur if the school superintendent and the school board support a program of educational reform that

— gives weight to the concerns of people involved in the reform process;

— uses a carefully thought-out program design that puts into effect the concerns and advice of those involved;

— provides adequate funding and policy support for a reform program that carries the process of improvement through to conclusion.

These steps require a local approach that is sensitive, involves exhaustive planning and informal negotiations, can adjust plans to meet local conditions, contains some effective staff development, and will commit years of consistent effort to pull together the diverse elements of a school district to support better schools.

True change requires a strong leader with a clear vision of how to focus school and community attitudes on a quality academic program; with knowledge of the roles school people play in school improvement, and the impact school culture and the community at large has on school quality; and with the ability to find, select, and put valuable, workable, new ideas into practice in such a way that people really want to use them.

While writing this book, I reviewed my own experiences in three school districts where I served as superintendent, compared my ideas on school renewal with literature on the topic of "reform," and exchanged ideas with many successful school superintendents and their staffs across the nation. This book is the synthesis of my study of the school culture and reform issues. Detailed information about my experiences and my visits to school districts appear in appendices A and B.

I would like to express thanks to many present and former staff members in public schools in Biloxi and Pontotoc, Mississippi; Sierra Vista, Arizona; Ardmore, Oklahoma; Social Circle and Richmond County, Georgia; Johnson City, New York; Springdale, Arkansas; and the Alabama school districts of Pell City, Jefferson County, Tarrant, Homewood, Hoover, and Vestavia Hills, who willingly answered many questions about how and why they made improvements in their districts. I found that everyone brings about changes in different ways, but there are common elements among the stories told by all successful innovators.

This book is dedicated to superintendents and school leaders who want to develop the traits and strategies necessary for building a community that values good schools.

Julian D. Prince

INTRODUCTION

Views of the reform debate have polarized. Advocates of restructuring argue the merits of placing more emphasis on teacher leadership — "bottom-up" change that will empower master teachers and put the burden of school improvement at the local level. Proponents of accountability disagree and advance "top-down" change — state-mandated programs involving teacher evaluation, curricula patterns, data-based decisions, and increased state and local student testing.

Superintendents are frequently trapped between the conflicting demands of these two views. They need to be able to respond to external mandates while at the same time encouraging teachers to initiate educational programs to improve teaching and learning. They must learn to build bridges; to involve themselves, the community, school board, principals, teachers, and parents as team players and full partners in creating an atmosphere that promotes student learning. Few superintendents are adequately trained for this difficult task.

Leadership is *the* greatest problem in reform. Time and again superintendents set out to reform the schools and then founder in their efforts. Sometimes they fail because powerful segments of the school or community are unwilling to make desired changes, but more often because they are being asked to do something for which they are poorly prepared. Divergent job demands, inadequate university and on-the-job training, and outside interference in the affairs of local schools are reasons superintendents give for their lack of success. In addition, many superintendents have management skills but lack information about theory and research on how schools teach students to learn.

Whatever the reason, superintendent tenure has plummeted over the last decade from an average employment of almost six years to less than three, scant time to bring lasting reform.

> There is nothing permanent except change.
>
> Heraclitus (540-475 b.c.)

Despite the current trend, there are some superintendents who manage a relatively long tenure and at the same time do achieve effective reform efforts. Is there a relationship between longevity and success? Are there techniques or systems of improvement that are better than others? If there are, what are they and can they be replicated?

I say yes to these questions. There is a natural way that schools, as academic social systems, operate. In this book, I will explain why this particular system is so difficult to reform, provide answers to the above questions, give examples of successful practice,

1

and tell how to go about effective school change. And I will explain the nature of the school culture and how to work with members of the culture to improve schools. Chapter one describes the school culture, defines the concept of systemic cultural renorming, and provides an overview of two further concepts, organizational development and general systems theory, that will enable you to deal with the existing culture. Chapter two describes five elements in renorming, and chapter three explains how to renorm a school district, discussing the technical aspects of the process and emphasizing time factors and the cyclic nature of events. Chapter four describes how one small district in Mississippi used renorming to reform its English program.

1

RENORMING THE SCHOOL CULTURE

THE SCHOOL CULTURE

School people live in a special atmosphere — their school culture. They understand that it is not theories learned at a university that govern the decisions they make in their classrooms, but their own beliefs expressed by action rather than word. For example, schools where academics are important are schools where teachers, principals, and community members value and reward such work.

In most cases, the superintendent can set the tone or direction of the district by his or her actions. But setting the tone is not enough. For change to last all the people involved must learn to believe in the superintendent's reform measures.

School districts that are educationally sound are that way on purpose. Effective schools have a strong commitment to district academic goals and a good evaluation system. Behind the goals, many different people are accepting responsibility for improving school quality. This combination of teamwork and administrator-guided organization works well. Often, however, district leaders who fail at producing a strong program, respond to public pressure for reform by putting most of their energy and resources into the latest trends as evidenced by the buzzwords reported in the educational press — merit pay, teacher empowerment, school-based management, restructuring — good, sound ideas that are destined to fail unless the school culture comes to accept them.

The hopeful person finds success where others see failure.

O.S. Marden

In *Corporate Cultures*, Terry Deal points out that the long-term stable characteristic of any organization is its culture.[1] If Deal is correct, the very quality of school life is a function of patterns of habit that control how people go about their daily business. Therefore, the cultural attitudes expressed to students about teaching and learning are vastly more important in determining the quality of an academic program than the physical and financial resources available to equip and house the school program. If we look around us we can see clearly that the schools in each nation are the product of a national consensus. Japanese, Russian, or American schools represent a sum of the cultural attitudes about the education of future citizens. This national consensus is modified by local attitudes. The quality of academic offerings in rural, inner city, or parochial schools is controlled by the attitudes of the culture that has the greatest impact on these schools.

In any instance where major academic improvements are planned to change a weak program, reform leaders must consider the cultural characteristics of the local schools, which determine and maintain the character of the existing program. Improvement can occur only as this culture changes.

Few administrators recognize the stabilizing influence the local culture has on efforts to bring about change. Confident, determined superintendents who believe that they are in full control of the flow of events in a school district improvement effort must acknowledge that they are not. To change schools, they must work with the attitudes and norms of the school community. The potential for assertive leadership to improve schools exists, but the superintendent does not have the command of the school culture. The culture is in control of its own destiny. In order to accomplish major changes, a substantial portion of the school community must understand and support any new procedures.

DEVELOPING THE ESSENTIAL ATTITUDES

It is characteristic for any culture to regulate the behavior of its members by demanding conformity to standards acceptable to the community. This stable characteristic is often identified in educational literature as a problem called resistance to change. But resistance is not so much a problem as people's attitudes. Leaders who seek change often don't recognize the depth and importance of the existing attitudes and norms − the present conditions that determine what is acceptable and what is not to the school culture. In a school district, change occurs only when school people understand, accept, and adopt alterations into their day-to-day routines.

Therefore the entire school culture, its members, and their attitudes and norms must be a superintendent's continuing concern during the process of introducing reform measures. There is a logical reason for this. The entire school district will be influenced by, or will eventually become involved in, the change process. If most members of the school population are not ready for change, they will resist change. Piecemeal efforts at change − the buzzword programs − will be driven out in time by existing norms of the rest of the culture.

Change can occur across an entire school district when the school culture sets a common goal. Putting in place the goal and a sense of mission requires many people to share the same focus for their activity.

To introduce the idea that change may be considered as a process that can be managed by changing cultural attitudes, I have coined the phrase systemic cultural renorming (necessary jargon, but not as ominous as it sounds). Systemic cultural renorming occurs when school people and community members choose to operate under a different set of academic standards. I chose the word *systemic* because careful analysis of any school operation will reveal a repetitious systematic pattern of activity. A typical school program is a network of relationships where people share common insights about each individual's place and role in the organization. Each person is comfortable with these familiar relationships. Schools retain the same characteristics day in and day out over years; new people who come into the organization are trained (acculturated) to operate in a manner that is acceptable to the members of the system.

Renorming means changing the beliefs of a sufficiently large number of people in the school district (parents, community leaders, school board members, administrators, teachers, support personnel, and students) in such a way that these people consciously influence others to use new, different values as standards for judging what is quality schooling. If the school improvement effort succeeds, "success is determined in large part by the underlying structure of norms, expectations, and beliefs. . . . Like an individual's self concept, this . . . climate exerts a powerful influence on the behavior of . . . members and . . . determines . . . success."[2]

When a substantial portion of the school district's culture wants schools to improve, schools will improve. School improvement comes when school cultures are renormed, not reformed. Changed practice grows from a conscious choice to improve. In the local setting, this means the goals must be set by the total culture. And the goals are set according to group consensus of what represents effective school practice. This is a very different way of thinking about school improvement, and it creates a process rather than substituting some imposed solution — a consultant with a bright idea, some new method of teaching science, school within a school, modern mathematics, new regulations, merit pay.

In the renorming process, local people select curricula to fit the culture's goals. Their ideas are an important part of the process, and ensure that major improvements will occur as a widespread attitude develops that a better academic program will be beneficial and that the everyday roles people play support new developments. These two processes must occur within the natural operating system of the school district. Superintendents must see that they are dealing with a loosely structured system, an unseen sociological reality. Yet, they also must see that they can control events in the culture as precisely as a square dance master controls the actions of dancers as the set is called. And they will achieve this control using the school district's traditional structures (legal, financial, physical plant, technical, curricular, evaluative) as vehicles to support academic improvement.

The process of improving a school's performance is necessarily slow and disorderly. There are no quick fixes in changing a culture's systematic nature. Schools improve as the concepts people hold dear change. The focus of change is not grand changes but small, often within single classrooms. Author Richard Schmuck insists that for ideas to be of use they must guide daily activity.[3] As the culture changes, school people adopt a personal version of the leader's vision through an individual professional growth process. Improved schools grow bit by bit, as school people make small changes — until most of the culture believes in, and regularly uses, better academic procedures.

Ineffective educational practices are habitual. The way to break unwanted habits is for the people who have them to choose to change. To do so they must be provided with a supportive atmosphere in which to practice new methods. If effective practice is a valued community goal, even the weakest members of the educational staff will want to improve, and they will seek help. Support for individual staff members with ineffective methods in such an atmosphere will not be seen as a put down but will be accepted in the spirit given. The superintendent's role is to provide the kind of atmosphere where people choose to make their schools better.

THE IMPORTANCE OF CHOICE

According to author James March, service organizations, which include social service institutions and all types of educational organizations, are characterized by three general properties:

1. Organization members discover preferences on the basis of activity.
2. Simple trial and error is more important in choosing courses of action than planned change.
3. Individual participation in organizational functions is fluid, unpredictable, and based on attitudes of individual participants.[4]

March's third point reasserts my idea that positive attitudes of participants are critical in successful reform management. Major programmatic change would be easy to accomplish if leaders could tease out and deal with the hidden agendas of every individual. Obviously, this would be a difficult task even in a small circle of close friends, much less in a large, complex organization.

If March is correct, the basis for a process of successful and lasting change would depend on carefully organized activity to build good individual attitudes by allowing people to discover preferences by trial and error as a new course of action develops.

Work by Bruce Joyce and Beverly Showers, staff development consultants, shows that simple trial-and-error attempts by teachers to use radically different procedures generate individual success only if there is a support group of others simultaneously attempting the same techniques.[5] Joyce and Showers are proving this conclusively with their current work in Augusta, Georgia. (See Appendix B.)

Individual trial-and-error use of any new procedure without a support group produces a low level of individual success — about 10%. Several people working together have a better chance of success. The reason? Because individuals can exchange experiences. The successful use of a technique by one person can be adopted by others; a failure by one person can be avoided by others. In time, the exchanges of information will result in consensus, and a new group norm develops. The preference of the support group becomes the endorsed method of operation of individuals, and new techniques are successfully installed.

Fortunately, appropriate management activity can bring about the process of choice needed to renorm a school culture. This activity does not have to be hit or miss. Two concepts, organizational development and general systems theory, offer superintendents two excellent ways to build good attitudes toward choice and change. These concepts explain why organizations resist change. Understanding them gives excellent insights into which techniques are useful to change ineffective operations that are cultural habits.

SETTING UP A CHOICE PROCESS

ORGANIZATIONAL
DEVELOPMENT
Organizational development (OD) is a process to help organizations develop and change; it is a "coherent, systematically planned, sustained effort at system self-study and improvement, focusing explicitly on change in formal and informal procedures, processes, norms, or structures, . . . using concepts of behavioral science. The goals of OD are to improve . . . performance."[6]

OD provides ways to bring structure to the renorming process, giving leaders more control of the process than typically expected by trial and error. OD is a powerful sharing activity where people are directly involved in planning and implementing reforms. Professionals "move out from their self-contained classrooms and . . . take on new role relationships as team leaders and team members."[7] OD changes group norms by supplying an assortment of planned activity, which has been shown by research to elicit desired group behavior.[8] A typical OD sequence of events includes the following elements.

Gaining acceptance. People involved in the change must expect that the reorganization will be beneficial to them. A study group composed of a representative sample of the people to be involved in the change process examine what is to occur before it occurs. This gives them time to understand the implications for people and procedures and express these concerns to leaders.

Two-way communication. In a school district, a communication network must be developed that involves a representative sample of people from all levels of the hierarchy of the district, all schools, and all cliques. Selecting participating members of the group to be involved in communication to give a balance in each area is a critical leadership skill. During each phase of the change process, information must be shared on events to occur and when they are to occur. Who will do what and when it will happen are critical considerations. People must never be able to say, "I did not know that it was going to happen!"

Diagnosis. Data collection provides information about the group and raises questions about what needs to be accomplished (What do we need to improve?); what people think (Do you have any suggestions?); and what they want to happen (If we could change this, what would please you?). Problems are clearly defined. For example, if discipline needs to be improved, disciplinary problems are catalogued and people are invited to suggest solutions.

An action design. The type of activities that will be used to solve problems are worked out by committee members. Who will do what when is clearly indicated. Questions about training (Where will it be done? Who will do it? How much time will participants be involved?) are critical pieces of information.

Problem solving. Plans are put in progress, and individuals are given opportunities to discover preferences by trial and error. There must be much modeling of successful behavior. Clearly defined support groups must be in operation. Formal and informal data collection must be done as activity proceeds (formative evaluation). Procedures are modified on the spot when the group has better ideas of how the activity should proceed.

Assessment of results (summative evaluation). At specified times several assessment questions must be asked in the planning and communication groups: Has the intervention solved the initial problem? Has the organization responded favorably to the changes that have been made? Are individuals adopting the new procedures? What directions are indicated for the future?

These are powerful procedures. Each of them contains March's three elements, which can bring about change within the existing organization or culture. Unfortunately, these procedures alone do not provide a sufficient base of understanding necessary to modify the instructional program of a complex school district and to sustain improvements over the years.

Additional information can be obtained from the National Association of Secondary School Principals. They have developed a training program called LEADER 123, which is based on OD concepts. This program advises principals to use four key tactics to upgrade a school program: planning, developing, implementing, and measuring. These procedures can be learned. They do work. Understanding why they work requires knowledge of systems theory (see next section).

Renorming schools requires more than social service organizations making choices by guided trial and error. A school district is improved through the simultaneous interaction of many factors — attitudes, leadership, planning, curriculum growth, instructional materials, effectiveness of teaching, evaluation of student achievement and personnel, discipline, atmosphere, effective time use, staff development, policy design, finances, physical plant, community relations, and publicity. Managing items in this list goes beyond the technology of OD. Systemic cultural renorming requires more than successfully understanding how to manage the sociology of school districts. General systems theory provides additional insights as to *why* cultural patterns are so difficult to modify and provides the techniques to manage the complex interactions simultaneously.

GENERAL SYSTEMS THEORY

General systems theory is a way of thinking about the world rather than a theory in the strict sense of the word. Originally developed in the 1950s by German biologist Ludwig von Bertalanffy as a holistic world-view, general systems theory begins with the idea that the world is organized into complex wholes or systems. These dynamic systems — whether ecology, biology, schools, or factories — survive because of balanced relationships among the parts and concern for the environment. Emphasis on the parts is inadequate for gaining knowledge about the whole; and because the whole usually is not fully understood, respect and restraint are important in dealing with all aspects of the system.

Applied to education, general systems theory acknowledges the basic structure underlying the educational system and helps explain the effect of change on this structure. Calling for a systematic approach to school improvement should not be confused with trying to generate some industrial production model of schooling. As educator John Goodlad points out "schools differ markedly from factories. . . . [educators] . . . find no useful place for the factory model in seeking to understand schools, but [the other choices available to us] do not add up to a fully alternative model."[9] Goodlad feared the imposition of a factory mentality on school programs, and he was correct to do so. Schools are not factories. They are different, but, as systems, there is a similarity. Each is a com-

9

Figure 1

LEADER 1 2 3 — The National Association of Secondary School Principals' Approach to the Use of Organizational Development Techniques

LEADER *1 2 3*
KEY BEHAVIORS FOR PLANNING

- Identify the instructional leadership opportunity or problem.
- Get relevant information.
  - List key issues.
  - List possible information sources.
  - List possible causes.
- Identify what measures and criteria would indicate that the problem or issue is resolved.
  - Identify quality assurance measures.
  - Decide how to gain acceptance of the plan.
- Relate the problem to the "big picture."
  - Decide whether a long-term or short-term solution is needed.
- Develop an overall strategy.
  - Consider alternatives.
  - Devise a "back-up" plan.
- Identify needed materials and resources.
- Identify key personnel.
  - Skills.
  - Motives.
- Establish timeline, schedule, and milestones.
- Set a challenging, measurable objective.

An NASSP development program for instructional leaders.

LEADER *1 2 3*
KEY BEHAVIORS FOR DEVELOPING

- Set the direction and objectives for project.
- Recruit "team" members.
  - Get team members to "sign up."
- Secure participation.
- Ask for ideas.
  - Listen openly.
- Get team to work on tactics.
- Delegate tasks and subtasks.
  - Request volunteers.
- Set deadlines.
- Organize materials and resources for quick, easy access.
- Follow up on progress.
  - Reward effective performance.
  - Remove obstacles.
  - Revise plans as needed.

An NASSP development program for instructional leaders.

LEADER *1 2 3*
KEY BEHAVIORS FOR IMPLEMENTING

- Communicate needed information to appropriate persons.
- Follow your plan.
  - Start on time.
  - Secure/provide needed resources.
  - Stick to your plan — resist minor pressures.
- Collect "data" to monitor project status, problems, and delays.
  - Revise plan as needed.
  - Develop additional materials or resources as needed.
- Anticipate unfavorable outcomes and try to minimize them.
- Divert or diffuse unneeded conflict.
- Celebrate accomplishments with/of participants.
  - Milestones when achieved.
  - Project completion.

An NASSP development program for instructional leaders.

LEADER *1 2 3*
KEY BEHAVIORS FOR MEASURING

- Identify relevant measures.
  - "Objective" records, scores, and tallies.
  - "Subjective" perceptions, feelings, and concerns.
- Identify comparison groups.
- Establish procedures for reporting/updating project status.
- Collect baseline data.
- Implement project/program.
- Collect follow-up data.
- Compare pre- and post-measures.

An NASSP development program for instructional leaders.

plex organization that attempts to produce a product. However, after that point the similarity weakens.

Schools are far more complex systems than factories, and there are vast differences in the products generated by each system. For example, the time span needed to achieve a goal varies considerably, as do the ways in which a high-quality product is produced. It takes more than a decade for schools to turn out their "finished products." They cannot choose the quality of their "raw material," which changes each time students master a content area and move on to the next. Every year, each student reaches a new level of intellectual development. Factory raw material is chosen because it has consistent qualities. School raw material is not chosen. It is there.

The educational system is complex because of the constantly changing interactions between teachers and students, parents and community members, and because of the ever-changing nature of society during the 13 years that children are in school. For example, in 13 years there are an average of three administrative changes and many school board membership changes. There is no question that employees of many school districts see the system guiding their daily activity as more permanent and stable than its administrative or policy leadership. This perception creates problems. Why should the staff adopt new procedures if the administration will soon change?

Despite changing leadership, there are predictable *patterns* of reactions in similar situations. For example, administrators can transfer effective patterns of leadership from one district to another; consultants can work successfully in many different settings; and administrators and teachers can receive common training. A state curriculum can serve as a guide for thousands of schools, and standardized tests can be used nationally.

There are generic elements in educational systems despite varying organizational patterns in subgroups. Local norms affect the whole system's corporate behavior only to the extent that local knowledge is useful in predicting the behavior of population subgroups peculiar to a given area. Given these conditions, the coordination of the human and technical systems of a school district during school reform can be done methodically. General systems theory is useful in understanding school district reform because it blends technical considerations with the planning and behavioral support needed to change behavior.[10]

Open and Closed Systems

There are two types of systems, open and closed. Both systems can be described by the same related properties. An analysis of the closed system gives excellent insights into the scientific basis from which systems theory developed and a better understanding of how a collection of parts can operate as an organized unit. A petroleum refinery is an example of a closed system. It is a controlled, enclosed system of pipes, retorts, and cracking towers, where every variable involving heat, pressure, quality of crude oil, and chemical contents can be carefully monitored and regulated by computer controls. Managing all these factors determines the amount and quality of products produced. If the refining process does not work properly, the system can be analyzed scientifically and adjustments can be made to correct the problem.

Open systems are less predictable technically, but are based on identical scientific precepts. Open systems respond to monitoring and corrective activity, though not as precisely as closed systems. An example of an open system is a farm pond used to grow fish commercially. The same laws of science are operating within the pond as inside a crude oil refinery. The open system of the pond is more difficult to control because it has so many outside influences. It is "open" because it is exposed to the elements and its boundaries are not easily defined. It is sometimes difficult to determine clearly cause and effect relationships associated with any single factor inside or outside the pond. For this reason the pond is defined as loosely structured. Given time and appropriate analysis, the health of the farm pond as an operating system can be calculated when certain conditions are controlled, such as — the water level, oxygen content, temperature, pollutants, food, certain types of animal or plant life removed or inserted. If good-quality fish are the intended output of the farm pond, certain environmental conditions must be maintained. If the pond is not working as desired, an analysis of the elements of the system's ecology determines what must be changed to correct the problem.

School Districts as Open Systems

Human systems such as school districts are open systems. They operate on a loosely delineated cause-and-effect relationship. Though it may seem trivial to say so, schools operate on the same scientific, but loosely structured, principles as does the farm pond. The bounds of the school district community are not as easily seen as are the banks of the farm pond, but the bounds are present, nevertheless. Unfortunately, the scientific principals of human ecology in schools is not as scientifically researched as is the ecology of farm ponds. Despite this, research about open systems gives excellent insight as to how a school district can carry out a plan of improvement by use of systematic techniques. These techniques have to be tailored especially for school districts and can use principles that produce predictable results while doing so.

The section that follows gives an analysis of a school district as a system that is more than a sum of its parts. Understanding these relationships is necessary in order to understand why school reform is so difficult. When teachers resist a renewal effort, the resistance exists because it *must* exist. Resistance to change comes because of a process called self-regulation, which is the natural way any organized system maintains its very existence. Resistance to change is neither bad nor good; it is a fact. Resistance to change can be overcome by learning other characteristics and principles of systems that overcome self-regulation in a natural way.

Characteristics of All Systems

Seven characteristics are defined below. Each is illustrated with a quote from *An Introduction of Systems for the Educational Administrator*[11] and a brief discussion of how each relates to efforts to improve the quality of teaching and learning in the typical school district. As you read this section try to look for points where productive systems can be knocked off track by outside interference and points where nonproductive norms can be replaced by more effective cultural patterns.

- *Every system has a tendency toward natural decay (**entropy**).*

> All systems, whether living, mechanical, or conceptual, are subject to use, wear and tear, and malfunction. Only the most vital [closed] and open systems survive over prolonged periods of time.[12]

All systems degenerate with age and the passing of time. Maintaining motivation and energy through continuing staff development is a critical operation in improving a school program. No matter how comprehensive the initial training, or enthusiasm for the improvement, it is the correct use of the new procedures under long-term supervised conditions that produces lasting change.

- *All systems **exist in time-space** (Any description of a system is a history of what it is at a particular moment in time.).*

> All systems involve the transformation of energy [into] activity, . . . all open systems exist in a nonreversible time sequence. Systems are evolutionary and either grow or degenerate over a period of time.[13]

The existence of a system is real, but reality is a thing of the moment. Describing a system accurately can be deceptive. The data by which a system's qualities are depicted must be collected at given points in time. Analyzing this data requires time, meaning that the system is evolving while the analysis is taking place. The description made from this data is history at the time it is presented. This reality does not invalidate the description of the system, but does serve to emphasize the fluid nature of living systems. This fluidity operates only in one direction, forward in time. It is not reversible. The system improves or degenerates; the graph line representing its health always moves forward.

A combination of people working together "has a character that is more than the pooling of its members' personalities."[14] If a desired way of operation has developed in an organization, it must be constantly maintained if the system is to continue to operate in the same way. The chances of maintaining the use of new procedures are small without continuing staff development because old ways of working lurk beneath the surface. Past training and local cultural norms are most likely to be the forces that control the way people work together. The positive side of constant decay of an organization, however, is that the planner can make use of decay to replace concepts of little value with better ones by conscious planning and continuous staff development.

The question to be answered at the outset of reform is this: What is it we know about the history of this organization that will be of use as a tool in planning for the future? Superintendents must have some idea if the school board has a history of willingness to "stay hitched" in rough times; of working together cooperatively. They must know what will happen to their leadership if controversy arises; how union leaders might react when certain conditions are present; if individual school principals have a history of motivation to work for the best interests of children. Careful planning and evaluation of what maintained the organization in the past is essential.

- *Every system has **boundaries**.*

> [All systems have] more or less arbitrary demarcations of that which is included within the system and that which is excluded from it. . . . that point, or those points, beyond which the unique aspects of the system are no longer distinguishable.[15]

The school system is distinguished from other organizations by its method of operation, philosophy, vocabulary, and interests. Many identifying characteristics are human in nature (knowing, feeling, caring, sharing). Others are technical and physical, such as a kindergarten facility sized to house "three footers."

The boundaries of a school community are imprecise, yet boundaries can be recognized as the point where the vocabulary changes. School people have their own terminology to describe events that occur in schools. When they have to translate school terminology to explain what is happening, they can be sure that conversation is being held with people outside the bounds of the school culture. Outsiders will consider the specialized school language jargon.

The implications of a language boundary are profound to the would-be school reformer. The appropriate language is the connecting link to gain support and understanding from the community that supports the school system. Different vocabularies for the school and the world outside the school explain why it is difficult to share the nature of school events with the general public and recently elected school board members. Communication must be carefully crafted to properly transmit information about any renewal effort to the local school culture.

- *Every system has an **environment**.*

> [The environment is] everything which is outside of the system's boundary. Environment . . . is contingent on the definition of the system and may vary as the system's boundary varies.[16]

The environment influences the operation of the school system. There are two environments that control schools. The *proximal* environment is that set of influences out side the boundary of the school district of which the system is aware, and over which it can exert some influence (PTA groups, booster clubs, parental support, grandparents, advisory committees, school auxiliary groups). The *distal* environment is that portion of the community of which the school may or may not be aware, over which it exerts little influence (electronic and print media, an individual voter's attitude, a city council vote, changes in demography, state politics).

The people closely associated with the school system may see the need for a bond issue as part of a reform effort and urge its passage. Public reaction to this reform effort in the distal environment can become hostile. The reform effort can be blocked by an adverse bond issue vote because some vocal segment of the public does not understand or is resentful of the philosophy of the new program, or some leader advocating the program. Having no children in school to benefit from an improvement, older residents may work with enthusiasm against a tax increase. The key to build support for the bond issue is to allow forces proximal to the school to work directly with negative elements within subgroups that are distal to the school but proximal to the support groups.

- *All systems have variables and parameters.*

> Factors . . . affect the structure and function of the system. Factors within the system are variables; factors in the system's environment are parameters.[17]

Open systems are vulnerable to influence by both internal and external cultural events — informal conditions, requirements, norms, traditions, finances, prejudices. Events that the superintendent is aware of can be moderated by planning and negotiation. Staff development through OD activity is so very critical to school reform because it guides and modifies school district employee behavior and can readily influence cultural variables (those hidden agenda items!).

Advisory committees composed of community people are also critical factors in reconditioning school programs because these committees assist in identifying and moderating the influence of outsiders. They can see where parameters may influence community reactions and help avoid flash points that are obvious to those who know the community culture well. However, any variable or parameter impinging on the system will exert its influence in nonrational ways. The quality of planning enhances or moderates the influence of these factors.

- *All systems have subsystems (the working units of the system).*

> . . . system parts are themselves systems. Each part can be further divided into smaller elements, each of which has its own function and its own relationship to other components.[18]

Every system has internal systems (cliques, departments, groups, committees, networks of friends) that operate as small units within the system. Each member of a subsystem has essentially the same desires and functions. Subsystems have the same generic traits as do larger systems, including boundaries and specialized languages. Members of the athletic department in a school often have difficulty communicating with members of the English department. Each group has a different background of training and tradition. Each group has a different rationale for existence. Each has norms that guide the behavior of individuals within the subsystem.

> The tenacity of a school's culture lies in the power of norms, how well they are adhered to, and how resistant they are to change. Norms are shared expectations, usually implicit, that help guide the psychological processes and the behavior of group members.[19]

The language used by the English department may not successfully inform the coaches or the counselors. High schools are more difficult to reform than elementary schools because they have so many different subsystems, each with unique traits. Elementary schools are monolithic; often each teacher is in a self-contained classroom. To reform a high school requires planning how to communicate with each subsystem. This must be done with the specific language that will key each department to participate in producing its own version of the needed changes.

- *All systems are under the influence of **suprasystems**.*

> . . . as all systems can analytically and practically be broken down into subsystems, all systems are, in fact, subsystems to larger and more complex systems.[20]

School districts are under the control of some larger agency. This agency may foster or impede reform. Some state departments of education are notorious in their efforts to control events at the school level. School districts answer to the city or county government, the state department of education, and they are responsible to the general laws of the state and the federal government. These are formal parameters, often written into law and regulation. Ultimately superintendents must deal with the regulatory agencies. In time, regulations, laws, and taxation procedures may need adjustment in order for a given improved practice to continue as designed.

Principles of Open Systems

The seven characteristics above apply to all systems, open or closed. In addition, there are nine principles that apply to the loosely structured open system, which explain its nature and add additional insights into why attention must be given to certain procedures in school district reform. Again, the outline established by Glenn Immegart and Francis Pilecki serves as a guide. Each principal is identified by a quotation, followed by a brief description of the systemic nature of the school district.

- *School districts are responsive to **inputs and outputs** (consuming energy to make a product).*

> . . . open systems maintain themselves by exchanging energy and information with their environment. . . . action stimuli [are translated] into outputs — terminal results or outcomes.[21]

The open system depends upon and is responsive to its habitat. Inputs are stimuli (provocations, motivations, positive feedback, incentives, prods, fears) which activate the system. Outputs are stimuli (reactions, products, services) that the system produces as a consequence of its nature. The system's responses are regulated by the system's norms. If behavioral norms are not as effective as they should be, system energy — material goods, human activity, tax money — is consumed in generating poor responses (achievement, for example).

It is possible for a school to operate quite smoothly, yet not remove students from the at-risk category. For example, administrators may make the decision to solve the at-risk student problem. Confronted with externally imposed changes to correct this problem, teachers may successfully resist if they believe that "this type of child cannot learn." Input requesting improved teaching procedures is rejected because the new procedures are seen only as disrupting normal operations that are valid according to their belief system. This same group may change voluntarily to a new educational program given proof that past procedures were harmful to children.

- *Every loosely coupled system has a **steady state** (the ability to maintain equilibrium).*

> [A steady state is] the process by which a system stabilizes itself and its contents within a tolerable and even variable range of limits.[22]

An ineffective, backward school district may seem to be static, unchanging, stuck in the past; yet it is actually quite dynamic. Any system that appears static has to work hard to remain unchanged in a rapidly changing world. The reality of the system exists for only a moment in time and space. Its seeming constancy comes because its subsystems rebuild themselves in an accurate replica of their original state as they constantly decay.

Superintendents can take advantage of this dynamic condition to make positive changes in the way in which a school district operates by changing the norms of behavior on which the school faculty depends to reconstruct itself. In order to improve a weak school district, the management of the change process must be placed in the hands of a temporary structure (study committees, development committees), guided by new leadership, to produce and sustain a better school program.

Subsystems maintain equilibrium by selecting and screening energy and ideas from their surroundings through coordinated, collaborative, joint activity. Input from the environment may be random, even chaotic, but the subsystems can select useful material from a random collection of material and reject or neutralize those ideas that do not fit cultural norms.[23]

This explains why teachers' groups may willingly adopt certain segments of a reform package (higher salaries, lower class loads, teacher aides) and successfully resist others (a statewide evaluation system, merit pay, teacher testing). This is what John Goodlad means when he states that "the system, not education, drives the enterprise."[24] By willful choice of ideas, the system can quite successfully maintain a steady state of poor practice in spite of outside pressure. The human analogy is the person in love who can see no flaws in the object of affection because love is blind.

Superintendents can disrupt the steady state of poor practice of a school system only by demonstrating that the new ways are better ways. In this way, superintendents gain the trust and respect of the culture and give its participants good reasons to adopt a different, more effective, steady state. A renewed school system has the capacity to support the new system because of the new norms and the new steady state. High-quality school practice is sustained when "the adults to whom society entrusts children and youth in schools . . . [are] . . . connected to the relevant sources of knowledge regarding teaching and learning."[25]

- *Open systems are **self-regulating** (the system autopilot).*

> . . . the thermostat on a furnace . . . [is a] . . . classic example of this property.[26]

The steady state thermostats of the school district are the accepted cultural norms, those things people are accustomed to doing. This includes manner of behavior, style, and local custom. Norms guide people to accept or reject reform measures.

To illustrate this point, imagine that top-down reform activity is proposed for a school district to get more effective instruction for at risk youth. Faculty leaders are not in sympathy with the solutions proposed because they have heard from a nearby district that the new procedures cause lots of paper work. Despite willingness of some younger teachers to give the new ideas a try, the system is able to maintain its old ways by its regulating mechanisms. Older teachers guide the younger teachers by disapproving efforts to cooperate. Someone who will not toe the line may suffer isolation (the silent treatment, exclusion from lounge conversation, catty remarks) until the transgressor gets the message. Good intentions fail for lack of support, and for all the wrong reasons. The reform could just as easily succeed if subculture leaders brought pressure on peers to conform to more effective teaching practice.

Early in the reform process, the superintendent must keep renewal activity within the system's acceptable guidelines. This is accomplished by bringing the established leaders (not necessarily those appointed to leadership positions, but a representative sampling of those who are at the top of the pecking order of school culture leadership) into the change process. At a series of meetings, data are shown to illustrate there is a problem and that it could be improved or rectified by a renewal effort. This process serves two purposes. The first is to allow superintendents the chance to judge the local problems that change may amplify. The second is to reach general agreement about why new procedures would be better for youth. "People are more likely to carry out the actions called for by a decision when they understand the implications of the decision and when they have committed themselves publicly to shouldering their part of the task."[27]

Providing free interchange of information, opportunity to plan, sound reasons for making the change, and plenty of opportunity for feedback can give subsystem leaders the opportunity to install a new set of norms for the system, norms that are better for children.

In the early days of school renewal at Social Circle, Georgia, curriculum coordinator Martha Ralls would find articles about the types of changes the district was considering. The superintendent wished to get these fresh ideas on school research into the hands of teachers, so photocopies of the articles were sent to teachers in the envelope containing their monthly salary check. Each time this occurred the check was sent out a day or so early. A faculty meeting several days later was used to explain the significance of the ideas in the articles.

- *There are many different ways to solve problems in the school community (**equifinality**).*

> . . . open systems have the capacity to achieve identical results from different conditions or the employment of different processes.[28]

Superintendents and subgroup leaders must accept ideas and suggestions from committed faculty members. Not only is this a trust-building procedure, it is a method that allows natural trial-and-error choices to take place. There must be an expectation that a goal can be achieved by many different types of activity, which can be carried out in different ways at different school sites within the school district without damaging the integrity of the overall mission.

It is not necessary for good ideas to come only from leaders. However, it is important that leaders recognize that when a useful suggestion is received from a member of a subsystem group (athletic department, counselors, English department) the person making the suggestion may have been chosen to deliver a message that represents the norms and attitudes of that subgroup. Therefore, to ignore such an idea without fair consideration would be to snub the entire subsystem.

The primary consideration of a renewal effort is to achieve the appropriate goal. The leader who is committed to just one method of achieving a goal may

— miss a far more effective (and practical) way of achieving the desired goal;

— miss an opportunity to give a valuable staff member ownership of a portion of the renewal effort, and thus a stake in the process;

— miss an opportunity to say publicly that contributions of individuals at all levels of the school district hierarchy are appreciated and valued;

— miss an opportunity to encourage others to come forward with good ideas that "just may make this thing work"; or

— fail to allow adjustments to the renewal program that may be necessary to fit the program into each situation.

People in leadership positions in the middle management levels of the school hierarchy will jealously guard "their" turf. These turf guarders may not understand the principle that there are many ways to skin a cat. Be sure that there are ways that good ideas can percolate up from people below the middle managers in the hierarchy without being squelched (that's one reason for a suggestion box).

- *Every part of a loosely structured system contributes to the strength of the system — this is the concept of **dynamic interaction** (a chain is no stronger than its weakest link).*

> . . . the open system maintains itself through the dynamic interactions of functional subsystems.[29]

A spider web is an illustration of a dynamic interaction characteristic of an open system. Individual strands of a spider web are delicate. A single strand is too weak to capture a large insect. The web, as a unit, is capable of snaring and holding large prey. An insect in the web at any point transmits information to all segments of the system as all of the strands in the web contribute to the capture. Use of the web damages its fabric, which must be repaired for the web to continue its work.

The human interactions in subsystems are less visible than a spider web, but they are as dynamic. Though tenuous, people-to-people networks can support or resist a superintendent's efforts. For reform to be lasting there must be enough supporters who understand what is to be done and are willing to work cooperatively to put the new procedures in place. Individual leaders, who are selected from the various subgroups in the district, strategically placed, and working in support of reform are essential. John Burks, superintendent of Social Circle (Georgia) schools, states, "It is not necessary to have everyone on board to get reform to work. It is necessary to have the important people on board."[30]

Events that take place in an open system are not reversible. Inappropriate words spoken in haste may be regretted but never forgiven. A leader who slights a well-respected, informal leader of a subculture may inflame the entire school district. The web of interconnections will transmit a signal to all quarters that the boss is not to be trusted. Antennae will be raised to detect other evidence of unacceptable behavior to be cataloged for future use.

Key individuals at critical locations in the district provide support by continuing to use and support the reforms, building and rebuilding the support network throughout the district.

- *Feedback is a necessity in the operation of the open system (information about the system triggers reaction).*

> . . . the cybernetic principle. Feedback that encourages the subsystem to continue what it is doing is positive (regardless of whether what it is doing is considered by anyone to be good or bad), and feedback that discourages what the subsystem is doing is called negative.[31]

Feedback is not to be confused with gathering or examining data. Evaluation provides feedback information. Feedback is the response that activates the self-regulation thermostat. Information that triggers positive feedback in one subsystem may cause the reverse in another. As an example, suppose evaluation reveals that the complaints of English teachers about athletes being out of class are correct. This information, as feedback, would affect how coaches and teachers respond to the complaints.

Feedback may operate in two directions and can cause dissension. Suppose for example, administrators decide that an evaluation shows the kind of data they wanted to see. They are encouraged. They decide to stay on course with improvements. Their feedback reaction was positive. On the other hand, faculty members who are union members may read the input differently. They decide that their professional organization's interests are not being served by the new procedures. This feedback reaction is negative. If both parties are focused on matters of who controls, rather than what is good for children, stormy times are ahead if channels of communication are not open to allow discussion of the issues. Organizational development ensures that communication channels will be open at all times so that substantive issues can be informally negotiated before positions harden into hurt feelings.

It is possible for positive feedback on new procedures to cause problems. On occasion, school districts going through a renewal process get into trouble by moving too fast. Suppose the members of the organization are impressed by attractive publicity coming from a pilot program. This positive feedback inspires project leaders to allow the new program to expand beyond the central administration's or project coordinator's capacity to deliver planning, financing, and services necessary to make the project run smoothly. The backlash of negative feedback resulting from an inability to deliver services may be great enough to badly damage the credibility of the reform effort.

- *Progressive segregation (the tendency to develop subsystems) is always in operation in the loosely structured system.*

> Inherent in an open system's evolutionary development . . . is the system's own ordering of its components (subsystems) and their functional relationships.

21

> This . . . contributes to the system's ability to cope with the forces affecting it.[32]

The majority of the school district activity is ordered and controlled by subsystems within the school district. This trait is of immense value to superintendents and school leaders.

> Where administrators and teachers aim high and work together to mediate and link their separate worlds, where administrators stay committed, where there is pressure and assistance, where teachers use the innovation, are mutually supportive, gain professional development and develop commitment, there is a likelihood of success.[33]

The benefit of the progressive segregation process is that superintendents have the opportunity to place effective components (guidance, instructional resources, research, evaluation) in positions where there have been ineffective, inoperative, or no subsystems before. For example, school desegregation was a traumatic time in the Deep South during the late 1960s and early 1970s. Court orders tore apart familiar patterns of operation. Many school administrators used the chaotic conditions to restructure school operations in a manner that would never have been possible in their conservative communities under other circumstances. Making use of great community concern for the future to get effective planning accomplished, combined with the willingness of the federal government to supply funds for innovations, the restructured school district's subsystems came out of the chaotic period stronger than before.

- *Progressive mechanization is in effect in all open systems (given the passage of time specialized policies, rules, and regulations develop which facilitate system operations).*

> The open system . . . is able to adopt and use procedural and regulatory practices to facilitate its processing of work.[34]

The various subsystems of the school district — the human systems of departments, cliques, and specialized resource groups — interweave their operations within the framework of the curriculum, evaluation program, facilities, advisory groups, policies, financing, community politics, among others and support new developments in the school district.

- *An open system can control its own destiny (**negentropy**).*

> The duration and quality of life for the open system is . . . in its own hands.[35]

The tendency for all systems to run down (burn up the energy that is available to run the system) is a natural occurrence. Entropy, the process of natural outflow of energy, is a physical law (the Second Law of Thermodynamics). The open system has the ability to seek out new sources of energy and select for use those sources that keep it operating effectively. School improvements energize the school district because new ideas are exciting to school district employees. People look forward to trying improved ways of teaching. Excitement is contagious. An improving system draws more attention, and in doing so, draws new sources of energy from unexpected sources.

School improvement is an evolutionary process that, when properly directed, occurs consciously and willingly on the part of participants. Much time is required for change to occur and for participants to be lead by reason to accept changes. But school improvement is also self-perpetuating. Participants manage their own affairs and often bring in more energy than flows out. This is the desired outcome for any reform effort.

□ □ □

General systems theory is a way to characterize the properties of all systems into one set of generic rules.[36] I suggest that these rules, the characteristics listed above, are sound guides to use in understanding how to accomplish the renewal of a school district. Careful planning, good leadership, adequate communication, staff development, and the development of consensus with the passage of time provide ways for new ideas to become new cultural norms within the subgroups that make up the school district culture.

2
RENORMING ELEMENTS

There are five major elements in the renorming process:

- visionary leadership
- middle managers as enablers
- a network of informal leaders (principals, teachers, parents, business leaders, elected leaders, and students)
- steering committees
- centralized planning and evaluation

In order for the process to succeed, all five must operate simultaneously, although not necessarily in an orderly sequence.

Swedish educator Mats Ekholm studied factors that affect development and found that disorder occurs for the following reasons:

> The school development process is not usually linear by nature. It seldom fits in with technological, rational intellectual structures. Because there are so many processes going on simultaneously in a fabric of social interactions, entire "bundles" of change appear at once. These changes are sometimes interlinked and further the course of development. Sometimes they counteract each other and the development process comes to a standstill or is obstructed.[37]

The leaders of the school improvement process must accept as their major role to change attitudes that are essential for the culture to adopt reform. Without attitude change improvement cannot occur. Top-level leaders of all factions of the school community must be involved in the proposed changes. The more new behavior that is required, the more involved the leader must be in the procedures.

Adopting Ekholm's logic that even under the influence of the best attitudes, cultural change appears technologically irrational, it follows that some person in a responsible

Most human organizations that fall short of their goals do so not because of stupidity or faulty doctrines, but because of internal decay and rigidification. The grow stiff in the joints. They get in a rut. They go to seed.

James Gardner

role in the organization must be able to state the nature of the desired change and monitor the course of the five arms of the process.

Human considerations, and primarily attitudes, are the driving elements of the reform mechanism. They provide the framework, the loose structure, the classroom, in which adult education occurs in the school district on a grand scale.

VISIONARY LEADERSHIP

Visionary leaders are able to convey ideas new to the culture in a consistent, enthusiastic, and practical manner so that information may serve as a vision of trends and changes in society and of new ways to educate children. A vital part of the leadership role is developing credibility throughout the process within the culture of the school district. Effective leaders can build bridges between ideas and implementation. They can apply ideas to local circumstances, using logic that will work with members of the local culture. They produce a plan that makes sense to the majority of the people who will implement it. There should be a sound rationale provided that these new activities will be beneficial to the education of children. They draw people who will implement the change into the process from the start.

Effective leaders also build on the historical background of the school district. Regardless of the strength of the local program, people have some pride in it because it represents their community, their children. No matter how brilliant the proposed new ideas, or how bad the current system, every idea should be presented in a manner in which people get a chance to choose a personal method of employing the new techniques, with peers and leaders modeling the proper use of concepts.

ADVOCATE YOUR VISION

Leaders who successfully guide reform must be able to communicate the critical ideas that can be used as checkpoints in time of confusion or serve as a constant reminder of the course to be followed. It helps if they have charisma as well. Tom Peters and Nancy Austin outline the leader's role this way:

> Attention, symbols, drama. The nuts and bolts of leadership. More is called for than technique. You have to know where you are going, be able to state it clearly and concisely — and you have to care about it passionately. That all adds up to vision, the concise statement/picture of where the [organization] . . . and its people are heading and why they should be proud of it. . . . The issue here

... is not, then, the substance of the vision, but the importance of having one, per se, and the importance of communicating it constantly and with fervor.[38]

If the visionary leader of the renewal effort is not the superintendent, then whoever is must be authorized to implement the new procedures with the full approval and visible support of the school board and the superintendent.

SERVE AS ROLE MODEL

Effective leaders must express new, desired behavior through modeling. They must not be detached. A sure formula for failure is to ask people to do something they cannot do. People learn best when they see and practice new techniques. Superintendents can demonstrate that the new procedures are important by attending training sessions, visiting critical sites, and hearing progress reports.

If change is desired by the leader, he or she must be personally involved in the change activity. Finding time for participation may mean developing skill at delegating predictable, repetitious, tasks of management to the central office. Routine procedures that are already operating properly can, and should already have been, assigned to knowledgeable technicians. If it is important for the staff to learn new procedures it is also important that the superintendent lead the changes.

SPUR PEOPLE TO ACTION

Use your enthusiasm for your vision to keep others focused on reform effort. Bruce Joyce's summary of the role the leader plays in school improvement is a powerful metaphor "a battery-operated, portable cow prod."[39]

MIDDLE MANAGERS AS ENABLERS

Middle managers have a vital role as enablers. These are the nuts-and-bolts people who handle the critical details of centralized operations. They can handle details in such areas as personnel, special education, counseling, staff development testing, and evaluation, freeing up the superintendent for more district-wide planning.

Middle managers must be used cautiously while change is being implemented. In no instance should they be allowed to shut the superintendent off from a free flow of ideas from school principals. Effective implementation of a program requires constant interchange and feedback of information. Direct access to critical information about the progress of change is essential. Normal channels of communication probably will not be sufficient. Too often bad news is sanitized for the leader. When the superintendent directly monitors critical changes the process will likely violate the existing behavioral norms of the central office culture. Central office staff must be retrained to accept this new behavior. The more directly information can be delivered to the superintendent, the more effectively the change process can occur.

STOP CENTRAL OFFICE
INTERFERENCE

Central office staff members can unintentionally inflict harm on school achievement by undermining the local school's team attitude. Teachers should not be required to serve more than one philosophy of operation. Any teacher or staff member in an individual school, regardless of the special area, should be under the direct control of only one person. Logically, the school principal must have effective command over the care, direction, guidance, and correction of his/her school staff. The principal must be free to remove those who do not perform up to generally held expectations (and to expect the necessary moral and legal support when this happens), and to select and reward professionals and staff personnel who accept and fit into the philosophical framework established as John E. Chubb suggests:

> Well-intentioned, outside control of school personnel runs the risk of undermining the coherence and cooperativeness of the school as a total entity and of discouraging the delegation of critical professional discretion to teachers. . . .[40]

Chubb also found that

> [school] organization may be shaped by things more removed from day-to-day operations — particularly by the way schools are controlled. . . . outside control may also systematically affect performance, by encouraging or discouraging effective school organization . . . this tends to occur in proportion to the amount of control outside authorities exercise over school affairs. The more control a school has over those aspects of its organization that affect its performance . . . the more likely it is to exhibit the qualities that have been found to promote effectiveness.[41]

Supervisors who demand excessive paperwork can cause principals to consume time needed for instructional supervision. Unfortunately, the reason that most supervisors, or assistant superintendents meddle in the local school affairs is because their job description empowers them to do just this. If district practice allows supervisors to enter buildings and exert unilateral control over some matter, this should be corrected by new job descriptions or modifying policies that allow such interference.

DON'T USE
INDUSTRIAL MODELS
OF SUPERVISION

Rigid line-of-staff supervision, that of a strict hierarchy, is an industrial model of supervision. This organization should not be imposed on a population which is highly service oriented. It can hurt academic performance.

A school's success depends on its local character. To damage this spirit under the guise of school improvement is an error. Goodlad and Chubb show that central office intervention may well be at the root of some serious academic problems in larger school districts. William Firestone and Bruce Wilson found negative correlations between supervision pressure and school performance. Chubb showed that supervisory interference can drop achievement a grade level in large districts.[42]

(Note: There are times when the superintendent must take a position to impose a top-down solution to a school problem. For example, if a court order enjoins a school district from following certain procedures related to the placement of special education students, the superintendent must make sure that the court order is followed. Superintendents must also recognize that though this is a time in which mandated practices can be justified, mandating such changes in all other circumstances must never occur without the support and advice of those affected. The commonsense approach is to recognize the difference between teachers being required to do something by mandate and doing the same act willingly because they understand why the particular change must occur.)

KEEP THE PRINCIPAL
IN CHARGE

If the vision of reform involves loosening central office control over local schools, make sure that principals have enough autonomy. School board policies and administrative guidelines must be carefully reviewed to determine how they relate to supervisor/principal links. If principals are not allowed reasonable autonomy in school operation then the superintendent's behavior requires action to loosen the bureaucratic reins. Board policy revision is in order. Rewriting policy and job descriptions backing this specific school improvement activity will be the type of involvement demanded of the superintendent to show support for the new ideas.

Supervisors should use their professional skills to observe and comment to their hearts content. They must not be allowed to step in and usurp a principal's authority to control day-to-day operations. Supervisory corrections of staff members must be confined to appropriate evaluation reports. The principal should make the corrections. If the school does not have a good principal the chances of the school being effective are severely limited. No amount of supervision can correct this problem.

The principal's role in the local school is critical to district success. Principals are in control of the local school situation, but this does not mean that they are independent of the coordinated activities of the district. Principals must be in charge of the process of preparing children enrolled in the school for the next rung up the educational ladder. This process must necessarily be coordinated with that of the overall mission of the district. This is done by principals building two links within the school district: bureaucratic links, which are formal enduring arrangements, defined by job descriptions; and cultural links, representing the accepted modes of cooperative behavior of a group of people.[43]

Principals set the tone for the unspoken agenda for the school. There is also good evidence that teacher/principal cultural links are the most powerful forces in controlling local school improvement. If teachers believe that their principal can lead them into forming a better school, they will willingly cooperate and enjoy the process.

Principals must know how to determine what is going on in the classroom. Principals who enjoy sharing in the teaching/learning process will usually be effective instructional leaders. They place a high priority on going into the classroom to see what is occurring, and become involved in a dialogue about teaching. In this way many principals learn from their strong teachers many valuable skills. In my own experience, I found that

- Principals should enter classrooms frequently to see what is occurring and to have a dialogue with teachers about what is found there; the principal must use a carefully thought-out observation form to objectively record teaching actions (without interpreting behavior while collecting the data); a long stay each visit is not necessary, but dialogue about what was seen is essential (hold judgment until what was seen can be talked about);

- There must be incentives for principals to enter classrooms, in terms of job descriptions, with times for visits specified;

- Principals must be given encouragement and support from other principals as to how effective visitation and supervisory practice can be carried out;

- Principals must be given training in how to follow up a classroom visitation in order to encourage more effective teaching practice;

- Principals must understand what assistance is available when classroom visits reveal problems.[44]

REMOVE WEAK PRINCIPALS

If central administrators are convinced that the principal cannot do the job as instructional leader, then the principal must be replaced. Each school must be led by a person who is able to place instructional leadership in the forefront of priorities. It is foolish to continue ineffective leadership if it is an article of faith that schools should be improved. The principal as an instructional leader is the most important person in school improvement.

A NETWORK OF INFORMAL LEADERS

CREATE A TEAM
SPIRIT

At the time this book was being prepared education publications contained many comments about teacher "empowerment." Unfortunately, some of this rhetoric pits different factions of the school culture against each other. However, successful communities of people best perform complex functions as team members. Firestone and Wilson call this relationship cultural linkage.[45] Teamwork puts no segment of an organization at a disadvantage. Teamwork excludes no segment of the group from participation in decision making. Any decision by administrator or union contract which works to this end is improper.

INVOLVE
TEACHERS

Existing knowledge about what needs to be done to improve the educational program is often an untapped resource in school districts. Wise leaders can find ways to draw from their staff knowledge about how to improve the academic program in the local schools. Interestingly, offers to provide such knowledge are often provided to administrators despite any effort to elicit it.

Will classroom teachers come forward and voluntarily work at school improvement? Joann Jacullo-Noto determined that teachers identified as leaders who were attending summer sessions at Columbia University were naturally different than other teachers.[46] She found in these teachers "a concentrated degree of teacher leadership behavior," which made them different from other teachers in the following ways:

- They talked about change, how difficult it is to teach other teachers and to reach out to state and professional organizations, as compared to most teachers, who talk about their students and their class.

- They talked about their role in the public schools. They see parents as allies in establishing their reputation as teachers, as compared to most teachers, who view parents as outsiders and adversaries.

- They made themselves known to people in power, as compared to most teachers, who remain anonymous in large groups.

- They established publicly their subject knowledge and pedagogical competence publicly, as compared to most teachers, who display their competencies only to students.

- They talked about individuals with "position power" whom they knew. Through such

31

contacts and other work these teachers saw themselves as system-wide change agents, as compared to most teachers, who think of creating change within the confines of their classroom.

- They were energetic and competitive, as compared to most teachers, who do not act competitively.

I have found many classroom teachers willing to involve themselves with the power structure of the school district. These people will be involved in school improvement even if it means working actively to remove what they perceive to be an ineffective administrator. The members of such informal coalitions will be drawn from across the hierarchy of the school district and will work, unpublicized and frequently unnoticed, as an informal network to influence the academic environment of the school district. Obviously, the wise and perceptive leader will recognize such a force and use it to make positive contributions.

The teacher contributors to informal advisory networks most often wield substantial influence in the district, but have no formal administrative position at any level of the school district. In Sierra Vista, Arizona, we found a classroom teacher, a former union president, who was influential enough to have her version of the instructional section of the school budget adopted over that of the superintendent. Later, this situation had a severe negative impact on the superintendent's ability to successfully lead the school board. The conflict could have been avoided if the superintendent had asked the teacher to serve on his team.

USE INFORMAL
LEADERS

There are informal leaders in any organization who are willing to work for their ideas. Their agenda may be hidden and informal, but they are willing to negotiate. To do so they seek out people who will listen to their points of view. These people, in concert with those who think as they do, will work with or against the administrative structure of the school district, depending on how they perceive their leader's attitude. The people in this subculture come from all levels of the district. The group, if properly empowered, has influence that will reach into every aspect of the district organization.

DISCUSS THE
SCHOOL CULTURE

Capable go-between personnel (supervisors, principals, and teachers) in the administrative network who are trained, and are willing, to implement the leader's vision must become key players in consensus building. They must understand how members of a human community (the school, its school district, its setting) work together to build general agreement that can remain stable through change. They must be able to identify and to draw representative teacher leaders into the planning process, reassuring them that they are full partners in reform measures. School staff must accept that a better school program takes concerted action. This attitude will help them in the renorming process.

STEERING COMMITTEES

There must be procedures to draw people from all segments of the school community. Subgroups already exist. For a school improvement program to succeed, a formal steering committee, or committees, must be developed to tap such groups. Formal committees must be designed to include a representative sample of the informal leaders mentioned above. The school board fits into this category. The board is composed of leaders representing different groups in the community. The type of support that the school board provides school personnel in the change process therefore is critical for success. The crucial difference is that school boards have the authority to support, needlessly delay, or destroy the process of academic improvement.

In Sierra Vista, Arizona, an excellent staff development program was completely derailed by internal conflict within the school board. By the time the board members had fought out personal and factional agendas, the momentum the school district staff had developed was completely destroyed, the administrative team scattered to other districts, and the school district had to begin again with new leadership.

In Richmond County Schools, Georgia, reorganization of a badly divided school board (after a prolonged court battle) provided the atmosphere for a major reworking of the instructional program. In Biloxi, Tupelo, Springdale, Pontotoc, Social Circle, Ardmore, and Johnson City there is a history of smooth transition of power and continuous board support of administrative actions.

The school board member who uses his/her personal agenda or the agenda of a special interest group ahead of the overall welfare of the school program can completely wreck the delicate balance needed to develop a good academic program. Keeping the necessary level of commitment to improve the entire school program is extremely difficult when the membership of the school board changes rapidly. Each time a new school board member assumes his/her position, a period of intensive private, and often public, negotiation is necessary before the board as a unit can begin to move forward with a united front on the issues which are necessary to support an improved academic program.

CENTRALIZED PLANNING AND EVALUATION

The local school district policymakers and superintendent must avoid reflexive response to problems, including the tendency to use political expediency and nonproductive cosmetic solutions to stem public hunger for quick and easy fixes. Too often accolades are given to a single school's star program, or to some some isolated activity — a school within a school, or a consortium where colleges and schools work together — which operates as long as it is funded by foundation or federal funds, to assure us that "schools are improving." Such token effort will not do. These efforts do not improve total school districts and are not changes that last.

Responsible long term fixes require that the entire school program, K-12, improve. Knowledge that this improvement is underway will come when an accumulation of statistical evidence shows that

— school dropouts and discipline problems decrease at the same time that daily attendance improves;

— achievement test scores increase;

— the number of students voluntarily taking more difficult courses in high school increase;

— ACT and SAT scores of graduates increase, and more graduates enter college;

— graduates do better in college as freshmen;

— non-college-bound graduates are employable;

— the public begins to comment voluntarily that schools are good; the rate of teacher turnover decreases;

— school levies are passed by the voting public.

MEASURE
PRODUCTIVITY

This fifth requirement also involves developing an improved educational delivery system that includes buildings, special spaces, books, the curriculum, technology, tests, evaluation procedures, and so forth. The last requirement points out that the "things" of schools become support items for an effective system of teaching and learning. Beans, budgets, and buildings are not the ends of the school program, but a means to an end. Choosing what constitutes better schools and achieving the right things for children supports the reform work of the central office of the school district.

3

How to Renorm a School District

Most of us drive automobiles with little knowledge of mechanics. As long as the car runs smoothly, knowing how to drive is enough. Let the car stall on a lonely road, however, and we wish we had studied auto repair.

By the same token, it is possible to be a school superintendent and operate the school routine without any knowledge of how to make major improvements in student achievement. Once the superintendent decides to do a major overhaul of the academic program, however, far more complex forces begin to operate. Improving instruction requires reworking the school culture.

GETTING STARTED

Getting school reform underway is deceptively easy. Usually superintendents give most of their attention to funding and planning. After starting a new program, many are lulled into thinking that the new procedures are going well. They successfully muddle through minor changes in school programs knowing little about the dynamics, or dangers, inherent in the reorganization process. Success in small matters breeds a lack of caution about the effort required to bring lasting change to an entire school program.

> The greatest revolution of our generation is the discovery that human beings, by changing the inner attitudes of their minds can change the outer aspects of their lives.
>
> William James

Then, two or three years later, public opinion and teacher resistance stop the project cold. Unseen and unexpected opposition bring reform efforts to an end because there was no process put in place to prepare people for the new procedures and the consequences of change. Evidence is strong that many superintendents who get into trouble in major reform efforts lack knowledge about the stress a massive school overhaul brings to the various factions in the school district.

Successfully implementing program improvement depends on the support of the people affected. This is an altogether different matter from the motivation required to *begin* reform. The spark to begin is fairly easily generated by foundation funds, school boards, and administrators. Motives needed to *sustain* improvement depend on people involved in the changes seeing the need for the new procedures and accepting responsibility for their success.

Draining the swamp means that the living conditions in the swamp will be changed. Agents of change who suddenly find themselves up to their eyeballs in alligators discover only too late that the alligators are fixed on doing away with the person who drained their swamp. The alligators were not heard from early in the process because the unsettling realities of the new program were not fully understood. But once the discomforts of change are evident to leaders of different factions, those inclined to resist find common ground to unite. Organized alligators on the march are very bad for the change agent's job security.

This chapter shows how to conduct a reform program focusing on the academic improvement of a school district. Techniques are recommended to encourage the initial willingness of the school culture to study and try out new ideas to improve the schools, and then to maintain the change process with sufficient momentum over a period of time long enough for new ways of behaving to take root.

Several considerations are critical in a successful reform program.

- New ideas must be attractive enough that, in time, they uproot the philosophy held by the members of the established school culture.

- Whether or not the effort is well or poorly led, individuals in the school culture will discover preferences about the new ideas through trial and error.

- The existing management of the school program is unable to generate the energy to make major revisions in its own nature unless forced to do so by dramatic circumstances — a court order radically restructuring the district, consolidation with another school district, or a fire which destroys a major facility, for example.

- A stagnant management can be energized to support a new culture by transferring responsibility for development to a new and temporary power structure, such as a task force.

- Management retraining must be a part of the process.

- Several years of effort will be required to incorporate major change.

- Proper administration of the reform process over a long period weights the odds in favor of the members of the existing culture participating in the process of choosing new, and better, methods of operating schools by personal experimentation and adoption.

- When new ways of doing business replace old ways, expectations for individual performance must be clearly stated. Staff members must know how to be accountable for the performance of students in their charge during change (they may avoid the responsibility of participating in the change-making process, but they cannot avoid an assigned duty which comes as the result of change).

Reform efforts have the best chance to succeed when effective management practice involves the entire school culture in making creative choices. Old management ways must be temporarily superseded by a new temporary management superstructure. This occurs only if a pool of productive ideas (from which choices can be made) is available to the entire membership of the organization. Members must be properly guided in making choices from these worthwhile ideas. Constructing this pool of good ideas is the leadership team's role.

SETTING UP THE STRUCTURE

School improvement is the process of convincing a school community of the need to use better instructional procedures. Administrators who wish to guide a community to better instruction must realize the process is so complex, and takes such a long time to accomplish, that the traditional administrative hierarchy and normal administrative practice does not provide a sufficiently strong cultural network to carry the process to successful conclusion.

During major school changes, a new network of temporary administrative relationships must be imposed on the established administrative hierarchy by the school district leadership. The new network is installed by appointing broadly representative task forces to accomplish particular purposes. These task force "committees" must be given the power and support required to make needed changes. The task force(s) must represent the district population. Fortunately, getting a school district to change does not mean abandoning past administrative patterns. What exists can be left in place for the time being. As changes occur, a time will come when there will be clear indications whether changes are needed in management practice. What is demanded initially is an expanded network that involves a greater range of options to energize *natural* leaders in the school district culture.

During the development of strategies that will change the nature of schools, day-to-day schooling can continue through the traditional administrative structure. This permits the planning and implementation of any new program to be moved outside regular managerial arrangements with no damage to the comfortable status quo. Under these special circumstances, planning and development are then accomplished by a more energetic network of many different individuals, including the regular district hierarchy. This expanded administrative arrangement allows information, aspirations, and hope to flow easily across the school district. The expanded structure also allows many more in the school community to buy into and actively support the transformation. In this necessarily temporary method of operation, the people who know a great deal about the technology or procedures to be implemented will command positions of responsibility regardless of their previous status in the school district.

In several school districts I studied, teachers, assistant principals, or middle managers in the central administrative staff have risen to powerful temporary positions heading study or development committees. In every instance the competence of such a person to head a committee justified a thoughtful alteration of the regular administrative structure. The superintendent understands that this temporary leader has authority to instigate change through a newly empowered role.

An expanded leadership network of temporary leaders generates energy that is not available in the usual district arrangement. Within this network, leaders will

— develop district-wide agreement on what needs to be done by choosing a clearly defined, commonly accepted mission;

— focus the activity of the subgroups (schools, departments, out-of-school support groups) on the chosen mission despite conflicting priorities or previous inclinations they may have held;

— manage the development of a new program to allow for trial-and-error adoption by individuals, while assuring that these personal modifications have the power to achieve the institutional mission;

— realize that there are no quick fixes or short-term solutions to the school improvement process; that patience, persistence, and consistency in building a new system are fundamental to success.

Each of these activities is detailed below.

DEVELOP MISSION
CONSENSUS

Consensus is critical to improving the program of a school district. Consensus is not easy to achieve because of differing self-interests of subgroups. Each subgroup — school board, central office, local school, department, committees, grade level, union, band parents group, PTA, parents from poor neighborhoods, and those from the suburbs — is a built-in pressure group. Each has its own priorities and ways to judge what it considers to be successful school operation. A subgroup acting independently, determined to get what it wants at any price, may act in a way to damage the overall school program.

Consensus building is a cultural activity involving many formal and informal negotiations. It creates a common ground of understanding of the across-the-board activity required to best educate students. The positive effect of such negotiations is to allow the school district to overcome the threat of independent group actions to achieve self-serving preferences. For example, in Sierra Vista, Arizona, a conflict between the school principal and the superintendent about who controlled what overwhelmed the ability of administrators to work as a team, sharing common educational goals. These conflicts had little to do with education as they were primarily power plays to diminish the superintendent's influence. The entire school program reform effort suffered as people chose sides.

FOCUS SUBGROUP
ACTIVITY

Gaining consensus on a mission demands the involvement of a number of individuals who have the ability to build accord across and within subgroups. John Goodlad and his associates have been able to demonstrate that in successful school cultures leaders of different factions work together as a team.[47] They do not work together in unsuccessful school districts. Team leaders must come from each subgroup found within the school district. These leaders must be creative people who make the education of children their first priority.

The successful school superintendent serves as a bridge between subgroup leaders. The superintendent who has skill at building links, a good level of personal emotional security, and who is willing to trust in the good will of fellow professionals is the right leader for this process. He/she must have enough self-confidence to ensure that each subgroup leader will be heard and encouraged to take part in determining the overall mission. Under such supportive leadership, leaders (particularly principals) will understand the nature of the school improvement proposed and its impact on their organization.He/she also will be able to create confidence among group members about the value of the suggested developments.

Principals in successful schools manage an intricate tangle of staff relationships. In such schools, staff members are held responsible for results, but within a supportive atmosphere. The principal communicates school standards and coordinates instructional activity.

District leaders produce much the same atmosphere in the school district as the principal does in the school. They produce consistency, a good network of communication, and good school spirit. Two areas of expertise are required to accomplish this — the skill to manage the personnel and technology of a changing school district to supply the necessary emotional balm for members of the school community during unrest; and the ability to understand the research and rationale behind the programmatic changes so they can confront roadblocks to reform efforts.

MANAGE
CHOICE

School managers must be publicly and privately committed to the chosen mission. This is difficult when subgroup committee members have the power to make decisions that affect professional lives. The superintendent and school board members, central office staff members, and particularly school principals, must model behaviors that support the decisions of special task forces. Line-and-staff administrative leaders must be perceptive enough to work closely with task force leaders. They support the task force by using their skill to smooth the way across cultural or social barriers of which task force leaders may not be aware. It is at this point that organizational development skills help administrators. OD develops a safe atmosphere for the members of factional subgroups to try out activities likely to achieve reform efforts. In addition, the direct involvement of leaders of small groups in the development and implementation of the new program is absolutely essential to provide these leaders with ownership of the new approaches.

BUILD A
DELIVERY SYSTEM

The technical nature of the existing school organization must be well understood. As I stated earlier, there is no need to abandon the traditional hierarchy of the school district. Stability is required as a point of comfort during times that will surely be troubled. There must be time for the members of the existing administrative structure to

— understand research-based knowledge about new procedures;

— match management behavior to support new developments (principals must understand how to supervise new teaching methods);

— help develop a rationale for change that states clearly the practical reasons for reorganization (for example, in Social Circle and Richmond County, clear cut statements have been made that children are not achieving as they should);

— organize insightful give-and-take planning involving formal and informal negotiations on policies, budget, personnel, facilities, and alternate ways to achieve the mission (reflection with action);

— put together a system to use the new procedures within the existing educational delivery system (teachers, physical plants, school climate, adequate budget, adequate materials) so that people can be successful by knowing what happens on Monday;

— develop measures to determine that goals have been achieved;

— communicate successes and failures;

— build a philosophy in which the local school culture is oriented towards pupil learning;

— support, but do not intrude; and

— encourage all people to commit to high quality academic efforts, particularly parents and business leaders.

Effective school improvement must be sufficiently sophisticated to overcome cultural problems, particularly the hidden agendas of turf guarding, fear of change, suspicion of new technology, and biases (whether racial, sexual, social, professional, or academic). At the same time the improvement processes must allow the new concepts to develop into personal choices because the quality of any educational program is controlled by cultural norms that represent the sum of individual habitual behaviors. Six or more years is a reasonable time for new cultural patterns to develop and become routine behavior.

PUTTING IDEAS IN A CONTEXT

The strategies outlined above may be put into practice through relatively simple modification of regular procedure. The difference is that regular line-and-staff administrators must be guided by, and cooperate with, task forces set up to bring about change. To do this management skills are needed that are different from routine practice. New skills include the ability to

— provide leadership opportunities for individuals from many different segments of the school community;

— focus policy guidelines and the administrative acts of the school district on achieving desired changes;

— generate staff development activity which assists personnel involved in teaching/learning activity to explore and choose personal professional options which will support the chosen mission; and

— provide specialized job-related training to assure competent, coordinated mission-related activity from all parties.

41

Each of these ideas is discussed below.

PROVIDE LEADERSHIP
OPPORTUNITIES

People involved in reform efforts must be able to contribute input as to how educational quality can be promoted. This input must be in place before the new program is announced. In Springdale, Arkansas, Elmdale Elementary School Principal Don Johnson constantly sends groups of faculty members to different school sites to "get good ideas." If the group likes some activity, a local committee studies how to modify the concepts for use in Elmdale School.

Members of subgroups must be involved in taking outside ideas and refining them to make the ideas work in the local school program. Those who might be affected by the new procedures (students, parents, central office staff) must also understand and support the changes early in the planning process.

FOCUS POLICY
GUIDELINES

There must be consensus about the academic outcomes to be achieved. Budgeting, administrative decision making, personnel practices, planning, curriculum design, and support services must center on helping students learn what should be mastered. Johnson City, New York; Augusta, Georgia; Ardmore, Oklahoma; Social Circle, Georgia; and Pontotoc, Mississippi school districts all have very carefully developed district curricular goals despite different philosophies of how to put good schools in place. Curriculum development must be more thoughtful than a knee jerk reaction to a problem area or weakness. Administrators often respond positively to an effective sales pitch — committing major resources to a new program on a short time frame. Only then do they consult a broad-based planning team to get them to back up a decision already made. At Springdale High School, many staff members were dismayed when they learned via the television evening news that their school was adopting a new program. Recently in Bessemer, Alabama, a three-year major effort to make the school district computer literate was announced with great fanfare — without a single teacher being present at a city-wide breakfast for community leaders, or for that matter, having been on the planning committee. This failure to achieve consensus is a sure-fire formula for headaches in the future.

ESTABLISH
PROFESSIONAL
TRAINING

If schools are to be effective, teachers must know how to evaluate the academic background of each student; what students are to learn, the level of achievement students are to acquire, and how to measure student success.

A new program has a serious impact on a competent teacher's effectiveness by changing teaching standards. Through staff development teachers can learn the rules of the new game. In Augusta, Georgia, Bruce Joyce insisted that schools be brought into the new instructional procedures as entire units. Then he carefully explained the new program and required a positive vote (secret ballot) by faculty members and the principal on whether or not to try the program. Subsequently each faculty member signed a pledge in good faith to become involved in training. Only then could each faculty, as a unit, enter introductory training at school district expense.

In the School-Within-a-School at Springdale (Arkansas) High School, a team of four teachers works independently of the balance of the faculty. Their goals are essentially the same as other teachers. Their approach to teaching is completely different from traditional techniques. The new methods — different daily schedule and methods of operation — are stressful, but the appropriate learning occurs because these teachers volunteered to teach in this manner. They know what is expected of them.

PROVIDE
STAFF DEVELOPMENT

Knowing what to do in a new program must not be left to chance. Job descriptions related to the new program must be clearly defined — from the superintendent's to the teacher's role. People on the firing line should be able to get clear instructions about the professional goals they are expected to achieve. Professional performance must be judged in terms of what is to be accomplished in relation to stated goals. There must be ample opportunity for discussions where individual hopes and fears are vented. In particular, leaders need to take time for informal visits to sites where changes are occurring. Listening to gripes and hopes of individuals on the firing line is very important. Responding to matters that may seem of small importance to an administrator (for example, not enough paper for the photocopy machines) is of great importance for some individuals, and therefore, for leader credibility.

As a new program develops, new cultural attitudes develop. Each new attitude, in turn, will require good planning to keep new programs viable. As time passes, new school programs require development of new job descriptions, new technology, and new subgroups. The new cultural conditions may be troublesome as new and old subgroups jockey for stronger positions within the school district culture.

MAINTAINING MOMENTUM

Many people believe planning and putting plans in action is a rational process. This attitude allows people to believe that good planning can bring about change in a short time.

Short time spans for major improvements may work for factories, but not for service organizations. The student of planning should carefully read *Productive School Systems for a Nonrational World*[48] to better understand the lack of direct connections between social service institutional planning and the procedures required to put the plans into action. There is a connection between planning and implementation, but it is tenuous unless procedures similar to those recommended in this chapter are used. The following quotes from this book illustrate the above points.

> The decision-making process in the nonrational model [of planning] does not conform to the neat, linear format inherent in the rational world. A wide variety of factors comes into play as final decisions are sought. Just as forces competing for organizational energy help shape issues receiving attention, individuals face competing claims for their own time. Most participants in the decision-making process juggle too many balls in the air at any given moment. Along with the various professional responsibilities jockeying for position, personal and physical demands eat away at the personal and psychic energy on the job. In effect, full-time employees of the organization turn out to be part-time participants in the decision-making process.
>
> Most of the time decision-making participants outside the organization also perform this role on a part-time basis. They have more leeway, however, to move in and out of the decision-making process without feeling accountable for their spotty participation. In sharp contrast, the dogged persistence of outsiders dominates the decision-making process because they can devote full time, even overtime, to an issue about which they feel strongly [discipline on school busses, drugs in schools, corporal punishment]. They quickly learn the slogan, "Persistence pays off."[49]
>
> By the time all the political, economic, and social forces come into play, the organization frequently is left with a limited number of options for serious consideration. Unlike the rational model [the theoretical planning model] with its full house of options open and available to the decision makers, nonrational reality paints a smaller picture, with fewer choices to make and with the best choices [often] removed from the picture.[50]

Public schools, social service institutions "owned by the people," often suffer from interference at the implementation stage. Some segment of the populace (professional or general public) will attempt to exert control over matters on which they have strong feelings. It makes no difference to a pressure group whether their attitudes are educationally or philosophically "right" or not.

The quotes above show that schools have two natures. One trait consists of tangible items — employees, programs, budget, and buildings. This nature of the school program deceives the planner into thinking that changing the system could be accomplished by changing these elements. If tangible elements were the only matters to consider, then planning and implementing the strategies could occur in "a neat linear format." Each school district is, however, a loosely structured culture combining tangible and intangible factors. The tangible elements and the intangible culture interact to produce a system unique to each population. Therefore, the loosely structured system requires plans equally non linear in nature if its character is to be improved.

Time and a clear vision of what must occur in order to improve the schools are the trump cards that can overcome the nonrational forces that would get rationally planned improvements off track. If the chief administrative officer has a clear vision of what needs to occur, and sticks to this vision as the rational thread on which beads of nonrational events can be strung, a cycle of several school years can carry the school improvement process forward with telling effectiveness. Small annual improvements on individually recurring events can mean a great accumulation of changed practice over a number of years. As in the fable of the tortoise and the hare, the victory goes to the one who keeps the goal in mind.

School activities occur in yearly cycles. These activities can be divided into three categories: planning, implementation, and evaluation. Each category has smaller units or elements — activities such as staff development, curriculum development, public relations, supervision, measurement and evaluation, and so forth.

Figure 2 represents a generic planning model that could serve as a guide as a school district implements a new program. This model takes its form from similar designs in the Effective School literature. Despite its theoretically sound concepts, the model is linear and thus flawed. All of the elements of traditional planning are present in the design — a mission, coordinated planning, curriculum and staff development, and evaluation.

These divisions are convenient for scholars to write articles about. They are useful for graduate schools of educational leadership to assign course titles to, and they make good divisions of labor for assistant superintendents. But these activities should not be segregated into turf areas in an active school program. Unfortunately, in larger school districts these functions often operate as fiefdoms into which no other leader must tread (and woe be it to the hireling from staff development who attempts to help out in curriculum). This type of turf guarding is a tragic misuse of valuable resources.

School activities that are poorly understood one year can be studied, reworked, and better presented the next. This annual renewal function is exactly suited to the talents of a good central office staff. But each administrator must support the mission of the total school district. And each unit of activity must be supportive of and integrated with the whole system operation. Only in this way can the system operate to make the 13 years of schooling run smoothly for each child.

Figure 3 displays the elements needed to fit linear plans to a non linear system. Systems theory provides the basis for the concepts.

When combined, figures 2 and 3 produce an effective planning system and an excellent way to put plans into effect.

Figure 2

Planning, Implementation, and Evaluation:
Effective School Components in a One Year Cycle of School Renewal

Coordinated Planning Activity: design of strategy to achieve the mission.

Mission Statement: the development of learning goals

Design Program Improvement
—new board policies
—new administrative procedures
—negotiate new relationships where needed
—new job descriptions
—new planning committees developed as needed

Curriculum Development: deciding which skills, knowledge, or understandings will achieve the mission goals.

Weighing of Total Program Benefits in light of assessment done by planning groups.

Determining Responsibility for Curriculum delivery — consensus on who teaches what.

Redesigning of the Staff Development Program to improve human performance.

Staff Development: Training needed to accommodate human behavior to new program demands.

Determining Personnel Development Needs based on assessment of results.
—central office
—principals
—teachers
—support personnel

Selection of Materials and Supplies: budgeting, purchasing, placement of resources.

PLANNING

EVALUATION

Design of School District Evaluation Procedures to Measuring Achievement of Desired:
—knowledge
—understanding
—skills

Assessment of department/local school/school district achievement of predetermined goals

IMPLEMENTING

Summative Evaluation of teacher performance

Individual Teacher Planning:
—set goals for year
—design units of work
—devise daily lesson strategies
—design personal system of testing for student learning

Formative Evaluation of teacher with professional and peer support provided as needed

Teaching Students (classroom activity)

Teacher Assessment of Individual Student Achievement:
—skills
—knowledge
—understandings

Assume that the activity begins with a spring planning session. In this session a planning group determines to enter into a new program activity. Many people who are to implement the program are involved in curriculum planning, determining what materials and procedures will be necessary to put the program in place, as well as deciding how to judge if the new program is successful. From this activity individuals who will implement the program are given new job descriptions and trained how to do the new job. They get peer support while performing the new tasks. Carefully designed evaluation activity measures student achievement by gathering evaluation data. New staff development enables adjustments to be made where necessary. Policies and procedures are developed that will support the new procedures. The cycle begins again as the academic year comes to a close.

Figure 3
Non Linear Elements of an Operating System

Each non linear element may be found at any point at any time in a cycle of program development described in figure 2. All of the elements may operate simultaneously.

MISSION – The general goals. The members of a system who develop an idea own the new concept. People involved in any new program must develop consensus about what is to be accomplished. Members of different factions represented must develop these goals. Developing goals allows members of different constituencies to negotiate formally and informally. Jointly stating what will be accomplished produces a common ground of understanding between different groups that could not otherwise develop. The leader should consider the initial mission statement as a general guideline. The leader should prepare to negotiate the mission statement periodically to change the statement when new group consensus develops. During a cycle of implementing a new program, a new consensus may develop at any point or time.

INVOLVEMENT – Participating in development activity. A person who develops a new program assumes ownership of the program. Direct involvement in implementing a new program provides opportunities for school personnel to decide procedure by trail-and-error. The program leader must provide school personnel the opportunity to assume leadership, develop curriculum, and conclude who teaches what, where, and to whom.

SUPPORT – Bolstering the new program through many constituencies. Solicit different factions to back the new program. Such support may take the form of financial aid, promoting the new ideas with various groups, assisting teachers, subsidizing a portion of the program for which they feel the most affinity.

OWNERSHIP – The notion of ownership is found in each of the three previous categories and in local option. Participants own the new concepts when the ideas become the norms of behavior that guide their daily conduct. Participating in meaningful activity that develops the new program, breeds ownership.

LOCAL OPTION – Each local school unit, including departments within the unit, should be allowed to develop a unique program. The local program must be compatible with the overall mission statement.

FEEDBACK – Information that modifies behavior of program participants. Knowledge of how each element of the program performs is essential for success. Peer feedback, where peers share results with each other in a non-threatening manner, is the most powerful and useful type.

INSTITUTIONALIZING – Rewriting the policies and procedures of the school district to conform to new patterns of behaving.

MAINTAINING – Adjusting the way the new program operates to assure long-term success. Maintenance assures that new people who enter the program become good team members, that feedback is adequate, and that accrediting agencies and new legislation supports the new program.

USING ALL
THE ELEMENTS
AT THE SAME TIME   The following questions will help you maintain momentum in
                      reform efforts as you plan for and evaluate the activities of each
year's cycle. As you read, you may wish to refer to figure 2 to clarify the relationship
of the yearly cycle to the specific activities or elements listed below.

Develop a mission statement. Good ideas should be carefully stated in terms of broad
appeal to the existing culture. The following evaluation questions should be asked annually: Does evidence from surveys, media response, and community members' comments
indicate administrative and school board understanding of goals which the community
would like to see achieved — that is, is the primary mission appropriate, is it developing
properly? As a new ecology develops with improving schools does the mission statement
now reflect the newly developed, and more complex, behaviors characteristic of the improving school program?

Assign responsibility. In any plan of improvement it is important to decide who is
responsible for what. Are leadership positions assigned to the best informed minds, regardless of the position in the hierarchy? State clearly and often who is doing what, when,
where, and why; how much can be spent, and by what time. Were job descriptions well
written? Should a better leader be chosen? Is it the common consensus that we have the
right people doing the right things?

Develop curriculum. The primary consideration of any school program is to assure
that students are being presented appropriately sequenced material in the proper framework for their developmental level. Does what is to be taught and learned remain appropriate for the conditions which now exist? Who delivers which part, when, and how
much? Does teacher feedback indicate that the curriculum dose for each grade level can
be learned in a year, or is it challenging enough? Are the subject matter connections
which are necessary for grade-to-grade, school-to-school connections properly made?
Is knowledge connected from one discipline to another — that is, does learning in one
subject matter field mutually support others? Does the new curriculum require different
delivery procedures than before? Must special administrator or supervisor skills be mastered
in order to coordinate the new activity? Are special teaching techniques necessary in some
areas? If so, who does the training? By what criteria will evaluators know that the knowledge, understandings, and skills intended to be learned have been learned?

Select material to support the curriculum. A new program may or may not require
new materials. Chances are that anything touching a curricular area will require upgrading
as time passes. Are texts, supplies, and materials adequate for the change? What do teachers

desire to retain of present resources (books, media, supplies)? What new instructional supplies are needed? Are things getting to the right place? Where will funds be located for new media? Will new storage, cataloging, distribution be required?

Prepare for evaluation of student achievement. Proper assessment requires that what is taught should be tested. What congruent tests must be developed to support the curriculum? Do tests accurately gauge knowledge, understanding, and skills described as objectives in courses of study? Can the data collected be used to support the professional activities of teachers? Can the data collected be used to aid decision making? Is any new technology needed to support evaluation of achievement?

Implement instructional planning as standard practice. Teachers, principals, and central office staff must know how to plan and what to plan for in all teaching/learning situations. Planned time use must match student characteristics. Does evaluation of data indicate that there is enough time being allocated to develop critical topics?

Check for effective delivery of instruction. Teaching episodes must be characterized by activity known to enhance pupil learning. Constant on-the-job interaction between teaching peers and supervisors should reinforce formal staff development activity. Does aggregation of data by special groups show equality of outcomes by race, sex, and SES group for critical skills objectives?

Use effective evaluation of professional practice. Evaluation of teachers and principals must be rationally connected with assigned job descriptions. Do students learn as expected? Do professionals support each other by peer evaluations?

Collect program evaluation data. Are tests congruent with curricular objectives? Are testing conditions correct? What does item analysis of test items show? Do teacher evaluations compare to performance in terms of student achievement? What evidence is there that higher-order teaching skills are being taught?

Evaluate student achievement. Are student outcomes (skill, knowledge, understandings) as desired? Are graduate follow-ups positive? What new directions are indicated?

Initiate administrative program review. Are good ideas producing the results expected? Is the climate good? Are other strategies more likely to achieve results?

Determine staff development needs. Does evaluation data indicate what can be done to help professionals become more effective? Training programs must be established where needed. Professionals must be observed and trained on the job to reinforce staff development activity.

Conduct long-range planning. Long-range plans are essential, but must not be taken as the final word, as nonrational forces can, and likely will, lead the best plans astray. Overlapping five-year plans is a good strategy — that is, the five-year plan is revised every year, with the new plan being adopted each year. Do leaders understand their role in executing these plans? What practices must be changed to get proper central office support for new procedures?

Redesign school board policies. Do present policies support reform? Are new policies needed to formalize good practice? What can be done to get board members to allow new programs to develop as intended despite political perils?

Forge new relationships. Community resources should be surveyed to determine untapped assets. Is the organization touching all bases which could better support program development? Should there be new cooperative business, community, school relationships: to support reform? to form new parent support groups? to establish a local foundation to support reform activity? to seek new taxes? Should the union contracts be renegotiated to be more supportive of effective procedures? Is there need to seek new state or federal legislation? Should efforts be made to forge new partnerships with other types of educational organizations?

☐ ☐ ☐

For a school improvement program to be viable, many activities must be implemented. If they are not, the school district reform efforts probably will be difficult to sustain over time. The elements in the following checklist establish categories of activities, directly tied to system theory, that enable reform leaders to avoid errors or omissions that could lead to failure.

Change Elements Checklist

Element	yes	no

Mission

Is there a clear statement of the long-term results desired? ☐ ☐

Does the mission statement include an effective explanation as to why the improvements are needed? ☐ ☐

Involvement

Are representative leaders from all subsystems in all areas of the school district active in developing the new procedures before decisions to implement have been made? ☐ ☐

Have representative leaders (administrators, principals, teachers, parents, board members, media representatives) been included in

— visits to other schools? ☐ ☐
— discussions of project feasibility? ☐ ☐
— defining the mission? ☐ ☐
— developing ways to achieve the mission? ☐ ☐
— suggesting how to do quality control? ☐ ☐
— accepting responsibility to champion the new ways? ☐ ☐

Support

Has school district leadership taken steps to provide a sense of security and a sense of achievement within the changing culture? ☐ ☐

Is there adequate financial support to accomplish stated objectives? ☐ ☐

Has knowledgeable leadership been provided? ☐ ☐

Is there adequate staff development for principals, central office personnel, teachers? ☐ ☐

Has training been accomplished by teams of peers working together trying out the new procedures? ☐ ☐

Is someone giving individuals and subsystem leaders specific training and backing as they work through unexpected problems? ☐ ☐

Ownership

Have participants been allowed to develop a sense of personal possession of the new procedures at the individual level? ☐ ☐

Ownership (continued)

Have participants been allowed to do trial-and-error investigations while working in teams with fellow professionals? ☐ ☐

Have teams of peers been provided opportunities to work together independently to discover better ways to make new procedures work successfully? ☐ ☐

Local option

Is the overall leader personally secure enough to accept the fact that there are many ways to achieve desired instructional outcomes? ☐ ☐

If good ideas develop at the local school of how the program should be modified to make it work (and whether it can achieve the overall mission) is the individual school staff allowed the option to modify the program? ☐ ☐

Feedback

Is there information necessary to determine how well goals are being achieved? Do evaluation procedures gather data directly related to program goals? ☐ ☐

Are there guidelines which show if the data collected indicate success or failure? ☐ ☐

Are there formal and informal open discussions of successes, failures, next steps, long-term hopes, in which all participate? ☐ ☐

When major or minor goals are achieved are there plenty of pats on the back, with sharing of the symbols of successful achievement? ☐ ☐

Institutionalizing

Are successful procedures worked into the fabric of the school district? ☐ ☐

As new and better ideas come from different sources are they recommended as viable procedures to staff members? ☐ ☐

As new strategies develop are they accompanied by appropriate staffing and new job descriptions to support them? ☐ ☐

Are good ideas formalized into new board policies? ☐ ☐

Are the new concepts worked into student, parent, and school staff handbooks? ☐ ☐

Does orientation for new staff members include the new concepts? ☐ ☐

Are staff members proud to say, "This is how we do it." ☐ ☐

Element	_____	*yes*	*no*

Maintaining

Maintenance involves proper modification of any American school system over several years to support the momentum gained from the activities above.

Are there annual efforts to

review, rewrite, and publicize the mission statements by a committee that is broadly representative of the school community? ☐ ☐

review job descriptions to assure that the important tasks to support the change process have been institutionalized into the various personnel positions? ☐ ☐

train people to adequately perform the new job descriptions that they have accepted? ☐ ☐

adjust the published curriculum to support annual changes in procedures? ☐ ☐

assure that there are adequate textbooks, media, and other materials in place to support changing curriculum demands? ☐ ☐

determine that tests and other measurements are available to assure that chosen instructional objectives are achieved? ☐ ☐

evaluate on-the-job performance by all professionals to determine the effectiveness of the delivery of the new procedures? ☐ ☐

summarize program outcomes using the data obtained? ☐ ☐

review and redesign administrative and board policies to adapt them to changing practices? ☐ ☐

negotiate or forge new relationships that would provide a strong base of support for the new procedures? ☐ ☐

4

RENORMING IN ACTION

This chapter describes a successful cycle of implementing a new K-12 language arts program in the Tupelo, Mississippi school district in the early 1980s. The development of the program may seem excruciatingly slow, but the reader must remember that this was not funded as a project, but depended on the available resources of the school district.

As you read the following account, you will note that the action jumps from one focus to another. Instead of proceeding in an orderly sequence as represented in figure 2, activities occur simultaneously, often because of nonrational pressures. These pressures have an impact on planning, implementation, and evaluation as deeper insights develop.

REWORKING A LANGUAGE ARTS PROGRAM

The activity begins several years before the fall of the year designated as year one. For some time informal discussions had been held between the superintendent, principals, teachers, and parents about improving the English program (*involvement*).* A curriculum writing effort in this area was not going well. The teacher committee could not agree on philosophy. The new program ideas crystallized in the fall of year one, when members of a parents advisory group expressed a desire to produce graduates who "write better." An English teacher in the advisory group commented on the difficulty of accomplishing this because of the size of classes and the existing curriculum "which emphasizes grammar and literature." She expressed how she thought this might be corrected. The advisory committee issued a call for an "improved English program with more emphasis in writing." This was done in the form of a paragraph in a mission statement (*mission*).

> To accomplish great things,
> We must not only act,
> But also dream,
> Not only plan,
> But also believe.
>
> Anatole France

*key words relate to elements listed in figures 2 and 3.

55

BEGINNING WITH
A VISION

The call for changed procedures was accepted. The superintendent, in a series of newspaper articles and position papers that winter, issued a challenge to revise the English program (*mission*). The wording of the questions were in terms of broad appeal to the existing school/community culture. "What would happen if English programs were to put more stress on writing?" Also that winter the superintendent appointed a study committee of teachers, administrators, and representatives of the committee who wrote the mission statement to determine how to revise the teaching of English (*involvement*). The recommendation of the broad-based committee was that more emphasis be given to writing. This decision was well publicized. Meetings were then held with representative English teachers.

Late in year one the matter of revising the "English" program was placed on the school board agenda (*support*). The school board, as a matter of district policy, "spread a resolution in the minutes" to favoring the improvement of writing as a district objective (*institutionalizing*). The action authorized the development of a long-range plan that would outline potential financial needs and possible policy changes (*institutionalizing*). The important result was to give legitimacy to the study effort.

CENTRAL OFFICE STAFF
STARTS THE
PLANNING PROCESS

In the summer between years one and two a format for planning was developed by the central office staff. This set many different activities into motion. A planning grant budget was developed. It proposed use of federal planning grant discretionary funds (made available to the school district through the state) for curriculum planning in language arts. This budget was approved by the school board and submitted to and approved by the state. Other likely sources of funds, such as grants from private foundations or business or industry, were investigated (*involvement, support*).

Early in year two the assistant superintendent for instruction was assigned the administrative responsibility for coordinating the development effort by working directly with the study committee (*involvement, institutionalizing*). A request for persons interested in chairing the committee that would oversee development was sent to the faculty (*involvement*). Job specifications indicated that there was no financial compensation for the position, though some released time was offered.

TEACHERS PLAY
A MAJOR ROLE

In the fall of year two, English teachers were selected to chair elementary and secondary divisions of the planning committee (*involvement*). Each had district-wide credibility as being experienced in using writing as a primary tool in teaching English. A high school teacher was chosen as the overall chairman. Subsequently, principals were asked to appoint members to the planning task force (*involvement*). Selection was based on a formula that included grade taught, level of experience, race, and teaching philosophy. Principals and a parent were included in the planning group.

In the fall of year two, a number of events began to happen concurrently. A local foundation entered the picture (*support*) and offered financial aid for the development process. Release time could now be assured for those directing the development effort (*involvement*).

The leaders of the planning committee, working in coordination with the superintendent and central office staff, agreed upon time lines for certain tasks to be completed (*maintaining*). A central office staff member was assigned to work with the teacher chairperson to prepare reports that would satisfy state and federal report guidelines (*maintaining*). Questions about what, when, where, why, how much could be spent on what, and by what time reports were expected to be clarified to the satisfaction of all (*institutionalizing*).

OUTSIDE HELP

Funds were provided in the state planning grant to employ the part-time services of a knowledgeable outside consultant (*support*). The committee members agreed on the consultant. Once chosen, this person had the complete backing of the superintendent and school board to use his/her expertise to resolve disputes (*local option*). Little was left to doubt. The planning committee, working under the assistant superintendent, had responsibility for program design, the project budget, and decision-making power on the K-12 curriculum and teaching materials (*institutionalizing*). This planning committee was empowered to operate for the entire academic year two (*maintaining*). Rule-of-thumb operating guidelines set for the planning committee included presenting plans to the school board in the winter of year two; developing early budget planning for year three; setting goals for writing curriculum revisions by the summer of year two and implementing a pilot program in year three; long-range planning for full implementation in year four.

CONSENSUS BUILDING

The planning committee's initial document was short. It was a scheme to improve English with greater emphasis on writing. Committee disagreements revealed that the initial conversations about the new program were causing great stress (*involvement*). As a result of the anxiety the members of the committee agreed to take a course in linguistics in the spring of year two. It was to be taught by the consultant to discuss the issues (*support*). Graduate credit was awarded to twenty people. The same local foundation supported the tuition for the teachers taking the course. By the end of the semester-long course some informal agreements had closed philosophical breaches dividing the committee (*local option*).

BUDGETING BECOMES CRITICAL

Running concurrently with programming planning were matters related to district operations. In the winter of year one a number of tentative decisions were available for policymakers on budget needs for curriculum development (*support*). A curriculum development budget was set to began July 1 of year two (*institutionalizing*). Also, based on the position paper produced by the committee, a small grant of funds was sought from a second private foundation to pay directors for the elementary and secondary curriculum writing efforts, and to pay teachers for extra time to do the initial curriculum writing (*maintaining*). The request for these summer development funds were bolstered by a grant from yet another local foundation (*support*). These two foundations promised additional backing if the planning process would be extended to other school districts by sharing curriculum materials and training to disseminate the concepts (*maintaining*).

THE CURRICULUM COMMITTEE

At the end of the specified planning period, the spring of year two, the planning committee was reorganized and reempowered as a curriculum development committee (*maintaining*). The state planning grant using federal funds was reapplied for and approved for the third or, "pilot" year (the reason for the quotes will soon become apparent). The same administrative arrangements, leadership, and membership — with only one defection — were kept (*local option*).

The committee, through subcommittees, planned who would do the summer writing to flesh out the freshly developed planning outline (*maintaining*). The committee chair was given the authority to employ committee members up to 80 hours during the summer of year two for the writing effort. Writing was done at the convenience of the teachers employed (*local option*).

In the summer between years one and two curriculum writing took place (*institutionalizing*). Teachers, led by the committee heads, detailed what was to be presented and learned at each grade level, and what the relationships would be between grades (*local option*). The committee agreed to the ground rule that the consultant would be allowed the right of veto, after consultation with all parties, if the consultant believed the committee was off track with the curriculum writing effort (*feedback*). The writing proceeded smoothly. Cooperating teachers apparently enjoyed the effort. The resulting material was brought to the larger committee for review and rewrite frequently (*feedback*)! Outline questions answered were, What is taught when, where, and how? and, How do we know it has been learned? The committee members were careful to identify differences between new and old curriculum material (*local option*).

A LOGICAL COURSE OF ACTION

A third level of planning was also in operation — how to put the program in operation (*institutionalizing*). In the winter of year two a decision was made to pilot the effort with two teachers in each elementary school and two teachers in each secondary school. This decision was reached because of the cost of replacing texts and concern that the new curriculum materials might need revision (*local option*). All work proceeded with this plan in mind.

The development committee, working with staff development personnel and the staff development director, determined what new skills were to be emphasized in staff development before the pilot year began (*maintaining*). While all this was occurring, and before the pilot program actually began, teachers requested the opportunity to take yet another a graduate course in how to write (*support, local option*). Again, a private foundation would support the cost of the training (*support*). By the time this round of training was over, half of the English teachers in the district had taken this particular course. Late in the spring of the second year, requests for teachers to be involved in the pilot phase of the program went out (*local option, involvement*). Far more teachers volunteered than could be accommodated. Participants were chosen from the volunteers.

NONRATIONAL CONSIDERATIONS

At this point (late in the curriculum writing summer) a new set of expectations related to the teaching of English began to trigger unanticipated activity. It appears that the change process changed gears; different influences (*involvement*) began to influence the rational planning process. Unanticipated intense lobbying arose from several different subgroups. English teachers insisted that the size of classes should be cut to aid in paper grading and many English teachers not selected for the pilot group wanted to use the new curriculum during the pilot year. Furthermore, parents wanted the new procedures to begin immediately. The unexpected demands were neither bad nor good. They sprang from the nature of new operating norms beginning to impose their character.

NEGOTIATING TEACHER CONCERNS

A major decision reached by the curriculum development committee was that if the changed teaching techniques were to operate successfully English classes must be smaller (*institutionalizing*). A group of parents requested that no English class in grades 7 through 12 contain more than 22 students and that total teaching loads be no larger than 100 students per day (*support, involvement*). Groups of English teachers began low-key, but intense, lobbying for smaller class loads. Frankly, school administrators blanched at this development. The budget was tight they pleaded — the opportunity to locate new sources of budget funds looked bleak. These facts were communicated. This response was rejected. New cultural desires, based on the goal to make written communication a district goal, required a new pattern of student assignment (*local option*).

A joint school board/parents planning group was assigned the responsibility of tackling the problem of class size, essentially a problem of finance. The decision was soon reached to request that city sales tax revenues would be diverted to this effort (*support*). Through a small political miracle, enough city funds were made available to accomplish the class size reduction goal suggested (*involvement*).

A second major unanticipated consideration was that many English teachers wanted to be in on the implementation of the new program; in fact, by summer's end of year two, virtually every English teacher requested to be a participant in the new program (*local option*). In effect this would eliminate the pilot year. Due to the publicity given the program, and the high hopes expressed by teachers involved in writing the curricular materials, parents began insisting (*involvement*) that the planned pilot study year be junked. The request (really, demand) was to involve every student in the program by the beginning of the third year. Hence, rational planning yielded to a shock wave of nonrational pressure when school board members recommended that the program begin immediately (*institutionalizing*).

LOGICAL CHOICES

In early August as year two closed, after curriculum writing had been completed, the superintendent called an emergency planning session of teachers, principals, parents (from the local foundation), and central office members. This group met to debate whether to approve full implementation of the new program involvement (*institutionalizing*). They reached the following decisions about the English classes for year three:

- implement plans as quickly as possible;

- distribute the curriculum materials in sufficient quantity to serve all teachers;

- provide at least a classroom set of new textbooks for each teacher;

- lower pupil teacher ratios in 7-12 English classes;

- expand the staff development phase of the program to involve every English teacher; and

- make other types of supportive materials available through foundation funds.

Under the circumstances, the nonrational limited options worked. If the school administration had forced the teachers to work under those conditions there would have been serious repercussions. Given the choice to proceed in this patchwork manner, satisfied the teachers and principals that the program was fair to everyone (*involvement*). Happily, test results at the end of year three satisfied all that the initial year worked satisfactorily.

MAKING THE PROGRAM
PERMANENT

Long-term maintenance of a program requires targeted support. Once any new program is underway, and appears to be working successfully, its continued success depends on planned efforts to maintain it. Successful program maintenance relies on having the correct upkeep procedures in place in the regular school district instructional support system. The next section deals with technical mechanisms available in the typical school district. As each segment of support activity is described, the narrative will drop back in time to match the thread of events of regular school operation with the narrative of the previously described development of the language arts program.

Providing materials: Sometimes making do is the only thing to do. New ideas require support of appropriate texts, tests, materials, and technology (*support, maintaining*). These items were only partially ready for English teachers in the rush to implement the program in the late summer of year two. Originally the development committee had chosen to deal with the known shortages of funds by piloting the program first. Earlier in year two plans were made with the business office and school board to use limited funds to phase in needed material over several years. These plans set limited priorities for purchase and placement of materials. A timetable was set for the completion of each step. As has been noted this plan, which seemed sensible, was junked for immediate full implementation.

The nonrational nature of the decision to skip the less costly pilot year caught the district unprepared to supply adequate materials. The decision was made to make do by emergency budget funds, reallocating textbook money (unfair to other departments — negotiation was required to take some of their funds), some foundation funds, and support from a publishing house. Fortunately these emergency plans worked.

Planning for evaluation. The evaluation phase of the new English program was implemented in year three. Plans were that a strong evaluation segment would be continued with each subsequent year (*maintaining*). Data were needed to modify any part of the program during the curriculum rewrites for subsequent years of development (*feedback*).

Determining desired outcomes. Mastery level standards were set for every grade level during curriculum writing (*institutionalizing*). Locally constructed, that is, teacher-made tests, were written to match the new curriculum (*feedback*). Measurement included levels of knowledge, skills, and understandings students should display. Tests were designed to assure that data collected would allow valid judgments about the overall ability of the school district to achieve mission and curriculum-planning objectives. Once the full program was in operation, classroom teachers provided much anecdotal information about the adequacy of testing procedures.

Measuring outcomes. At the outset of year three, samples of student writing were collected and filed for comparison with other year-end writing samples (*feedback*). During year three (and subsequently), data from many sources (achievement tests, locally developed tests, anecdotal data, before and after writing samples, student logs, results of competitive writing contests, parent reaction, subjective evaluations by teachers, etc.) were analyzed to see if students were achieving as desired. After each school year formal year-end evaluations compared achievement expectations to accomplishments (*feedback*). When desired results were not attained, the administration and its planning committees concluded they needed to make major program changes or to modify but continue as planned (*maintaining*).

Reports compiled from evaluation efforts resulted in formal documents for authorities and private foundations (*maintaining*).

Staff development. Staff development for teachers, principals, and central office staff began in the summer at the end of year two. The purpose was to teach how to plan for and present the new program. During year three principals were trained (*institutionalizing*) to do formative evaluation. They checked teachers' planning (*maintaining*). Doing this provided indications whether or not the teachers' objectives and use of teaching time were covering those topics agreed upon by the professional planning committees. At the outset the planning committee decided (*local option*) that the teacher might cover more material than allocated, and could cover the required material as creatively as desired, but that teaching the essentials of the writing program as outlined was a part of the job description (*maintaining*).

Modeling as a staff development activity. Staff development initiated at the outset of year three was primarily group lectures to familiarize teachers and administrators with the new materials (*institutionalizing*) and bring the new curriculum on line. Individual follow-up of this training was emphasized during the course of the school year by mini-clinics and visits to other teachers' classes (*support*). The best of these sessions during years three and four were open-ended discussions resulting from visitations in which teachers discussed what they were seeing (*feedback*) in other classrooms, or what they were doing to solve common problems. Individual performances by teachers were monitored and commended or altered (*feedback*) with special training where needed. The most valuable of these activities were modeling teaching sessions where "lead" teachers taught classes before observers and allowed them to question them about their techniques (*support, maintaining*).

Principals use teacher evaluation as a staff development activity. New evaluation data were gleaned to determine how to help professionals become more effective at teaching the "new" way (*institutionalizing*). Once the program was underway the principals' responsibility became that of determining that teachers were covering that material identified as essential. Formative evaluative materials for collecting data were designed for the principals to use (*maintaining*). They were trained in using these techniques. Evaluations by principals did reveal that individual teacher presentations translated into desired student achievement (*feedback*). Not all teachers were as effective at the new techniques as desired. Principals recognized who needed help and requested staff development activity where required (*support*). Constant on-the-job interaction between the teacher and peers, and between teacher and supervisors, indicated (*feedback*) that in the main, appropriate writing skills were being presented in the manner agreed upon.

Corrections from feedback data. Pilot-year evaluation revealed that additional staff development would be required (*maintaining*) to teach holistic grading techniques (judging a writing effort on merit for style and clarity of message) to get grading consistency before year four began. A serious problem in year three concerned teachers' inability to do holistic grading. Detecting grammatical errors was a different skill from determining writing quality.

In year three evaluations revealed that the program was effective.

Maintaining effective support services. The effort to improve English teaching was but one of the many school improvement attempts requiring central office attention, and was one of the desired program improvements fitted into long-range plans of the school district. New questions now had to be asked: Were all the new programs, particularly the language arts program, getting the administrative support deserved? Was the central office staff sufficiently involved in the new programs (*maintaining, support*)?

Evaluation energy was expended to determine if all administrators understood how to provide support (*institutionalizing, maintaining*) for the new English procedures. From this evaluation administrative changes were made where needed (*feedback*). Administrative handbooks had to be rewritten to adjust to the new procedures. The monitoring of district-level support is described below.

Maintaining support from policymakers. One problem with some school boards is that they may not stand hitched if pressures arise that oppose new program activity (*maintaining*). Their decisions often hinge on contacts with long-term friends or with political or business ties. The decisions made in such circumstances may greatly distress professional staff if they are based on political reasons rather than educationally sound rationales. This can occur particularly if board members are not familiar with what is being attempted. Consider the following scenario which might have happened (but didn't) during the early stages of the English program development described above:

> Occasional strained relations appear as the new program develops — that is, a well respected English teacher who has always prided herself on her students' mastery of "grammar" quits the planning committee early in the development phase. As the program gets underway, and she discovers that she does not like it any better than she thought she would, she begins to openly oppose the new program. She solicits support from several parents and friends of her age who believe that the old ways are the best ways. Several of her supporters write letters to school board members. Several others talk to board members individually, often calling the new program a dumbing down of school district standards. In this event the board asks for the issues to be discussed in a board meeting. The decision is made to do an independent board review of the concerns (*feedback*). After study the board discovers that the original position of the board to support the program was appropriate (*institutionalizing*). The development work done by the widely representative, duly appointed planning committee was well thought out. In this case the board members allow the program to continue to develop. There is good evidence that, despite possible political perils, the best interests of students will be served by continuing the new program. The board continued to support the new program because they accepted the new norms which the professional staff had put in place.

Finding new resources. Superintendents must continually determine whether the school district is touching all bases — parent groups, civic clubs, private foundations, private donors, business, and industry — that could support a reform effort (*institutionalizing*). New cooperative ventures may need to be developed with these organizations to get long-term program support. Some ways these organizations can support include: forming new parents support group (*maintaining*); establishing a local foundation to support a particular reform activity (*maintaining*); seeking new taxes to provide smaller class loads (*institutionalizing*); redesigning union contracts to be more supportive of change (*institutionalizing*); seeking new state or federal legislation (*institutionalizing*); forging new partnerships with other types of educational organizations (*maintaining*); developing new mission statements for other areas of the curriculum (*mission, maintaining*).

□   □   □

The events occurring in this activity involved nothing new, no "restructuring," no dramatic short-term activity which would excite a Carnegie group. The improved program happened because, over time, the people in the entire school culture came to see the need for a revised English program. Virtually every phase of the community became involved in support of the new developments. Note how this listing of events compares to activity suggested by the NASSP (figure 1) for developing a new program in a school:

- The spark which ignited the program was a comment made by an English teacher to a parents' advisory committee at just the right moment to get the committee to act favorably on a good idea (*mission*).

- The superintendent recognized that the idea was feasible and used the comments of the parents' committee to generate interest (*mission*).

- A group of teachers who would be affected by the change were pulled in to discuss the feasibility of the venture and give suggestions as how to carry out the process (*involvement*).

- The school board went on record as supporting the project (*support*).

- Funds were made available to free a knowledgeable teacher to oversee planning; this teacher was given the charge to develop an English program "just the way you want it to be" (*involvement*).

- A central office staff member provided support while the teachers developed the program and did the planning (*support, involvement, ownership*).

- Developmental funds from three private foundations were made available on a matching basis at just the right moment to solve critical problems. Those who made the funds available felt a sense of ownership (*involvement, support, ownership, maintaining*).

- Teachers were given time to talk out their reservations about the new program in a very professional atmosphere — a no-cost graduate course with university credit (*support, involvement, ownership*).

- A consultant was employed who was willing to let teachers develop the program and make corrections where necessary (*local option, support, feedback*).

- All curriculum development was done by a curriculum committee composed of teachers who would be affected by the program — this resulted in extra pay, for work done at their convenience during the summer (*support, involvement, institutionalizing*).

- Staff development was directly related to the job description and curriculum materials to be taught, the most important phase being the modeling of correct teaching behavior in the classroom (*support, local option, feedback, maintaining*).

- School principals were very involved in development of the new program, each at one time or another committing some of the school's resources to purchase supportive materials necessary to suit teachers' personal preferences. They were knowledgeable about what was to occur in the classroom and could do effective formative evaluation. They were free to develop modifications of the program in their own building (*support, owner-ship, local option, feedback, institutionalizing, maintaining*).

- Policymakers were willing to roll with the punches and take risks that the plans were sound enough to make the developments school policy (*support, institutionalizing, maintaining*).

- An effective program evaluation plan was in place to determine that what was supposed to occur actually did (*maintenance*).

- Evaluation data were available to make positive corrections toward continuing development of the program (*feedback, maintenance*).

These events resulted in renorming attitudes about how English should be taught in the school district. Given a good maintenance-of-effort program, there is no reason that the teaching of English should ever revert to the old, less-effective method of presentation.

APPENDIX A

SOME PERSONAL
EXPERIENCES

As a superintendent, I have found that some experiences helped develop the right conditions for stronger academic programs, and some did not help. I have listed examples below as illustration.

Ideas developed in one school don't go over well when imposed on another school faculty. As a young and inexperienced superintendent, I attempted to transplant methods of academic operation learned at one high school into another without doing the groundwork necessary to have such ideas accepted. I had spent six years improving the quality of a high school's instructional program. Decisions had been joint ones. The school was recognized as a sound academic high school and my election as superintendent of schools in a neighboring city was based on the recognition of this work. It did not occur to me that each new situation required its own rocky negotiations in order to hammer out an academic program. I pressed the new district to use procedures which were familiar to me but not to them. Even though the school board wanted changes, the faculty did not readily accept that different operating procedures were needed. Things did change, but grudgingly, and after much debate.

The real way that people do business is through the give and take of informal negotiations. Chester Karras, a nationally known negotiations trainer, points out that "negotiation isn't something reserved for diplomats and labor relations people. We all negotiate, and we all spend a great deal of time at it. We negotiate in business with the people we buy from and the people we sell to. We negotiate with our own bosses. We negotiate with our own employees. We negotiate in our personal lives time and time again."[51] Day-to-day work, jointly solving problems with school staff members, is the kind of give and take necessary to improve schools. Informal communication of this type is important because: it is a planning and fact-finding activity; it allows the leader to stick to the game plan, yet gain legitimacy for the plan because others have the opportunity to contribute ideas to the outcome; both sides can win, and goodwill and rapport

> The most powerful factors in the whole world are clear ideas in the minds of people of good will.
>
> J. Arthur Thompson

67

can be developed; both sides have a better chance to hit a target, because the target is a common target, jointly chosen; both sides can determine their strengths; and both sides agree to work together rather than oppose each other.

Negotiations are the essence of good team spirit — free give and take. Success was gained in the first superintendency by taking time to negotiate about things considered critical by each person involved.

Sometimes the most important job is to establish new ways to work together. My second superintendency was in the school district where my teaching career began. I knew the community well, but, unfortunately, successful patterns of past operations could no longer be employed. Old ways no longer existed. The culture had changed, and it was a time of great unrest. Academic matters had to be given careful attention, but school desegregation had to be accomplished also.

It was difficult to maintain a focus on academic matters. New ways of doing our daily business had to be learned. Success rode on restructuring the entire school program, academic as well as social. Several years into the process, I spoke to a national press association meeting about the process of education becoming a more scientific field of knowledge.

> Education today is in [a] traumatic era [of being unable to solve specific learner problems]. There are serious ills in our society today associated with the poor, which education should be able to modify. For some reason the application of our best professional techniques does not solve these problems which need to be handled. In education, we have many excellent generalities, but, unfortunately, the[y] . . . do not solve our specific needs.
>
> What, then, is a school as an educational institution? . . . [It] is a reflection of the community's social order. The school has as its purpose the exposure of the young to the society that the adults desire. The school equips the young to use the trade-tools of the society — language, mores, work habits — in an effective way in order that the society properly continue its existence. Where the desegregation of a society succeeds, it involves the solution of some of the most complex human social problems [which trouble our society]. To the extent that this is accomplished in my community, today, education is . . . successful.[52]

We had to find ways for people to work comfortably and productively with new cultural and educational structures while maintaining a sound academic program. This same process operates in any major readjustment of any school program. People will always be uncomfortable with new roles, whether they are academic or societal. A great deal of communication, experimentation, and sharing of concerns is necessary to bridge this uneasiness.

During desegregation we were fortunate that no one was an expert at finding solutions to the major readjustments. Good ideas on keeping the academic program viable were welcomed, even solicited, from *everyone*. Without any conscious thought about teamwork our central office administrators slipped easily into the habit of asking for help on different things — first on how to desegregate schools, then into seeking help on day-to-day operations in a computer-oriented world.

Asking for help, and accepting the help offered, is not a sign of personal weakness; it is a commonsense approach to finding solutions for complex issues. During desegregation, school leaders found it easy to seek advice. Concerned study groups were charged to come up with good, practical, affordable ideas to solve problems. As time passed, group problem solving focused on problem academic areas: how to improve the teaching of reading, computer-assisted instruction for mathematics, computer management of student records, education for higher-order thinking skills, and new approaches in vocational education. Group problem solving took time, but committees of parents, teachers, students, and administrators succeeded in helping the community build better approaches to teaching and learning.

Good natural leaders are found at every level of the organizational structure of the school district; find them and put them to work — everyone grows from the experience. During desegregation, the district spent four productive academic years (1967-71) tied by 2500 miles of telephone wire to a federally funded computer-assisted instruction (CAI) project directed by Patrick Suppes at Stanford University. The educational activities of 2400 children in six elementary schools had to be coordinated. Each day every elementary child participating in the program would sit at a clattering teletype machine to get his or her individualized computer-generated drill and practice by long-distance telephone relay.

Staff development procedures held people involved in the CAI project together. The first summer of the project 21 teachers and principals journeyed to Palo Alto, California, to receive training from Suppes and his staff. They learned the value of: sequencing a mathematics program, mastery of fundamental skills, and building higher-order skills. The teachers returned and trained others to model correct teaching behavior and to use an appropriate curriculum geared to pupil entry level. This cadre of local staff were dedicated leaders. They kept others enthusiastic, and the school district developed new ways to operate the school under their leadership.

Prepare public support by involving community leaders from the beginning — the school community does not end at school property lines. Our failure to make the CAI reform fully understood by the community killed the project. When federal money was phased out, our small district was unable to continue financial support for the project. Our school board enjoyed the national and international publicity, but they were reluctant to raise taxes to provide the $100 per pupil per year necessary to continue the project. We spent four years developing CAI as a viable instructional tool. This period should also have been used to convince the tax paying public to support the program that was producing good academic results. The school district administration did not bring the public aboard, and they were not prepared to support our expensive, yet workable, ways of teaching!

Programs might not transfer from one district to another — good human relations practice will. My "consensus building" style of management was transferred to another school district in 1976 and used for school renewal purposes. The district was already academically sound, but the board wanted us to upgrade student achievement with a curriculum coordination project.[53] Over 10 years, the project grew to include all aspects of the school district program, and a variety of committees were used to produce high-quality academic programs. During this period, school district professionals

— established, and constantly reworked, a mission statement;

— operated a superintendent's advisory committee composed of teachers elected by peers;

— created several different teacher/parent/principal study groups — evaluation, test development, planning, drug abuse, discipline, school plant cleanliness, support of special projects, and so forth;

— provided study courses on educational research for school principals and central office personnel, based on their job-related personal evaluations;

— put in place extensive staff development activities, which ran throughout the school year to include all district personnel (these activities were directly related to curriculum development, and emphasized effective use of time);

— extended summer employment to allow teachers to write curriculum and to assure that teacher input be the means through which new curriculum material entered the school district;

— trained teachers to do peer evaluations and support each other in improving teaching efforts;

— developed a local teacher-developed, criterion-referenced testing program with tests congruent to the curriculum;

— began data-driven program evaluation;

— developed continuous interactions with parents and business people;

- focused on discipline and improved school climate;

- developed a dropout prevention program that included instruction in parenting skills; and

- supported the development of a local foundation to provide funds for research and development.

All these were surface indications of deep community commitment to better education for the entire school district. These changes required the cooperative labor of many dedicated professionals, parents, and school district supporters. Ideas for program changes came from all directions, from vocational education to dropout prevention, and the superintendent became a broker of activity seeking funds for others' ideas.

School programs are not effectively organized and administered if left to chance. One of the most startling findings came from a survey of attitudes and practice in the teaching of mathematics. Fresh from my experience with one well-coordinated program, I analyzed mathematics teaching practices in the new district and discovered a lack of continuity in the mathematics program — in curriculum, teaching techniques, or what teachers considered to be essential. The consensus of teachers working independently of each other, when asked in the evaluation if this were true, indicated that the program was sequenced. Over 13 years of schooling, students could wander through a rainbow of ideas and practices in their mathematics training. Although the district had a commonly adopted mathematics text series and a district "curriculum," there was no continuity of program from teacher to teacher or grade to grade. Such dissarray of technique and purpose was eventually corrected only by a prodigious curriculum redesign effort and massive staff development — all of which had to be carefully planned, organized, and executed. We found these same conditions to be true in every phase of our academic program.

People who are excited about what is happening will pitch in and help if given a chance. During this time, change in one area inspired bursts of development elsewhere within the school district. School personnel were quick to point out that "old ways" were not adequate to support the new academic procedures they had designed and adopted. Each change in ways of getting teaching done required better support procedures from the school board and school district community. During these years, three bond issues for new construction were passed by vote margins of 92.4%, 92.0%, and 90%. The community was involved in the changes, had a stake in the success, and worked for success.

Effective school reform practices seems generic. During several consulting jobs, I experienced a sense of déjà vu. Strategies similar to those in my own district worked elsewhere, and I asked myself what was common about these experiences.

71

Each location had undercurrents of resistance, on initial exposure, to different academic procedures. Good communication was required to locate ways to commit individuals and groups within organizations to support change. Comprehensive staff development was always required. There was equal difficulty of measuring success in each setting.

Insights gained from the experiences above posed a number of questions:

- Although the type of reform goals were quite different at the outset, why did changing the academic approach produce similiar patterns of resistance across time in local school settings in the successful school districts?

- Why was extensive staff development so important in each site? Why were spurts of dynamic and wide-ranging activity involving simultaneous change on many fronts characteristic of the school improvement process?

- Which elements in the process are nonproductive; which are likely to bring the most success?

These questions became the focus of a study of school districts where I knew academic reform had taken root.

I conducted surveys concerning events during school improvement efforts at Biloxi and Pontotoc, Mississippi; Social Circle, Georgia; Sierra Vista, Arizona; Richmond County Schools, Augusta, Georgia; Ardmore, Oklahoma; Johnson City, New York; and Springdale, Arkansas. Impressions gained from the school districts listed above were compared to over 125 documents on the topic. From my review of the literature and my interviews with representatives from the school districts listed above, I made the following observations:

- School administrators, their boards, union leaders, public officials, and many who write for the educational literature apparently confuse changing the structure of educational programs with changing the quality of educational programs. As a result, many programs that are touted as innovations involve rearranging administrative, contractual, physical, or technical aspects of school programs while ignoring the real problem in poor schools — inadequate knowledge of the teaching/learning process, and lack of management skills to coordinate the academic program to provide instruction for children with a wide range of learning needs.

- The culture of a school district is a critical consideration in any process of academic change. How change occurs is well defined in the literature. The theory of the dynamics of change are well understood by specialists in the field. Many agree that academic improvement is made possible only by changing cultural "norms," and that the number of norms equals the number of groups that exist in the school district. School leaders

72

appear to have little knowledge of the cultural nature of the reform process or the ability to turn research into effective practice. Leaders in the districts I visited were aware of what worked and what did not, but their manipulation of "human" mechanics were often hit-or-miss targets of opportunity after some academic improvement process hit a snag (as most succeeded, obviously they found solutions). Special events were brought into play when there was "trouble." Initially very few saw, or expected, the interconnections between change events and attitudes of personnel until forced to recognize the linkages which were far broader and deeper than suspected.

- Evidence is limited on the time necessary to make new practice a standard. Successful school leaders thought "years." Ralph Tyler holds the opinion that it takes "six or more years" for reform to take root.[54] There is common consensus that surface changes happen quickly; acceptance slowly. Significant change cannot be accomplished in a short time.

- The culture of a school district is very complex. The ecology — the complex interrelations of attitudes, the roles people play, the impact of community sociology, and the physical, legal, and ethical interactions of a school district's life — is not well understood. Although *ecology* is a biological term dealing with the concept of the totality of patterns of relationships between living things and their environment, the concept is well suited to the human condition in the school community. An observer of a school scene may see improvement needed, but the people in the school setting are ecologically bound to the conditions which should be changed. Here, imposed reform, which causes unwanted changes in normal behavior, threatens the tranquility of daily expectations of the affected faculty.

- Researchers who desire improved schools may have addressed the wrong audience with their findings. There is a disturbing difference between literature on the dynamics of change published for university consumption and that for the common school leader. A search through educational administration magazines published in the past decade for articles on the mechanics of academic improvement shows few titles. During this time most school leaders (or those who write for them) did not write about the cultural nature of academic improvement. If professional magazines reflect administrator activity and interest, the administrator attention and efforts of most administrators is survival — board relations, personnel matters, union negotiations, school plant maintenance and construction — not how improved school academic performance requires improving the attitudes of people.

- Districts with long-term successful programs of improvement have years of stable leadership. Nationally, the tenure of superintendents is short. The time required to change a major school procedure appears to be about six to ten years. If average tenure is about three years, time for reform is not adequate.

- Many studies show that resistance to change is one norm of school society. Only under proper circumstances do norms change — for example, when members of the school culture see that there is good reason to change.

RENORMING ON SITE

Recently the leaders of the Council of Independent Colleges wondered what factors promoted exemplary education programs among their members. To determine this, they appointed a Taskforce on the Future of the Academic Workplace in Liberal Arts Colleges. This group found that characteristics of organizational culture at liberal arts colleges influence the quality of education. Eugene Rice and Ann Austin studied the characteristics of colleges in the survey population of 140.[55] They identified the 10 highest on ratings of faculty satisfaction and morale and found four key features of organizational operation in the 10:

- distinctive organizational cultures that are carefully nurtured and built upon;

- strong participatory leadership that conveys direction and purpose;

- a firm sense of organizational momentum — these colleges have a sense of an organization on the move; and

- the faculty's "unusually compelling identification with the institution" that incorporates and extends the other three characteristics.

Rice and Austin described teamwork, respect for fellow professionals, and a strong sense of mission. I found much the same characteristics in the public school districts studied in preparation of this book.

This appendix contains five substantially different approaches to reworking a school program. Districts chosen are Pontotoc City Schools, Pontotoc, Mississippi; Springdale School District Number 50, Springdale, Arkansas; Ardmore City Schools, Ardmore, Oklahoma; Social Circle City Schools, Social Circle, Georgia; and Richmond County Schools, Augusta, Georgia. Each shows many of the cultural, programmatic, and administrative characteristics that have been described earlier in this book.

> The essence of success is that it is never necessary to think of a new idea oneself. It is far better to wait until somebody else does it, and then copy it in every detail, except for his mistakes.
>
> Aubrey Mennen

PONTOTOC

Location:	Northern Mississippi
Type of District:	Small city/rural
Population:	4,723
Student Enrollment:	1,750
Racial Mix:	30% minority cultures
Per Pupil Expenditure:	$2,342
Students Receiving Free & Reduced-Price Lunch:	47%
Reform Area:	Staff development
	Strong, effective leadership
	Strong community mission

Demographic information about Pontotoc schools is not very impressive. The small city is located in a part of the nation legally classified as Appalachia. There are three schools, (K-3, 4-7, and 8-12) with a total budget for 1987-88 of $4,100,000. The total faculty numbers 97; 20.76 to 1 teacher-pupil ratio.

Mississippi's Education Reform Act does provide a full-day kindergarten with a full-time teacher's aide for every classroom for K, 1, and 2. Staff development, instructionally-oriented principals, a strong superintendent, and a sense of community mission are dominant characteristics.

What does get one's attention is high scores on the Stanford Achievement Test (ranging from the high 70s in the lower grades to the mid 60s in the upper grades), which are administered statewide in grades 2, 4, 7, and 10). Approximately 10% of the students in any grade tested fall below the 50th percentile. On two statewide achievement tests — The Mississippi Basic Skills Test (grades 3, 5, 8), and the Mississippi Functional Literacy Test (grade 11) — the school district will consistently rate in the top four of the 154 school districts in the state. Test results like these place Pontotoc as one of the top performers in all academic categories. This was not true five years ago.

In the spring of 1988, Pontotoc school principals read the results of statewide achievement scores over the public address system to students and teachers. A parent who happened to be present in one of the schools at the time said the reaction "was the same as if the football team had scored a touchdown, the only difference was that the students knew that each had helped make the score."

Superintendent Charles Harrison believes that the programs in his school district are well developed state-of-the-art activities which are highly divergent from teacher to teacher. We let teachers teach the way they want to. We stack the deck, though, with a testing program that matches the curriculum. The point is not that they teach alike, what we want is for them to get the results that we agree on as professionals are needed and attainable.

Harrison insists that you cannot do something to one phase of the school program without it affecting all other aspects of the school operation. "We have an overall target to have good schools. We preach that it costs no more to do it well. Whatever happens in the school district our task is to trade less desirable use of our time for better time use."

"Positive use of power" is Harrison's description of good leadership. His belief is that the school administrator's primary task is in the proper use of the responsibility given to the office. "My job is to help other people be more successful. If I can help every person in my district do his/her best then my reward is found in the good things which we all produce. My job is to be a broker of success."

During an interview, Harrison had the following comments about his district's program.

On the skill of the classroom teacher to handle classroom improvements:

If you were to need to repair a spider web you wouldn't do it yourself — you'd send in a creature that could build the web. Don't mess around in a teacher's classroom trying to make her or him teach a particular way. If the results are not good, keep after the weak teacher, giving help in developing better teaching strategies, suggestions, and modeling how to do research-proven methods until this person can get the job done — but let it be her or his way. It's your job to find a way to judge how good the results of teaching are if you are to get outcomes that are desired.

On assuring that students of different ability get a fair chance in the classroom:

A full-blown, high-quality testing program, which corresponds with your instructional program, is essential to your student body's academic success. Socioeconomic conditions have a great impact on the ability of students to learn. Teachers have to be responsive to this fact. You must have some way to disaggregate achievement data to determine what is happening here. If it is important you must know how students at various economic levels are achieving. If you can dig out this data you have a good chance to intervene to help students who are not getting it.

That what is to be taught cannot be left to chance:

Your curriculum has to be organized professionally and effectively. This organization is not something which you can just let happen. Teachers should develop it. It should be frequently reviewed. It must be the teacher's idea of what needs to be taught. Kids must learn things that are agreed upon to be important. These are curriculum imperatives — they are the stuff of everyday instructional activity.

That level of certainty of something good happening must be guaranteed:

There must be a level of assurance for the entire community that the money being spent in the schools is done in a good cause. People must see and believe that good things are happening for children. You don't do this with publicity. You do it with an effective plan where the complete atmosphere is right. When that happens it is not difficult to get the funds needed to improve a quality program.

What makes the Pontotoc school program different from most small rural school districts is dynamic staff development activity. Pontotoc's program has a strong base in training staff in research-proven practice with massive doses of support and follow-up.

Pontotoc principals are spending more time directly involved in curriculum and instruction. Each keeps a daily log to document his/her activity. Principals report that they are spending more time with instructional matters because they feel more qualified to do so. Several programs that have been used as training models are the Fenwick English curriculum mapping model, Carolyn Evertson's research on classroom management, and Madeline Hunter's ideas of teaching as decision making.[56]

Teachers report that there is a substantial change is the amount of time needed to teach district curriculum objectives as opposed to what comes next in the textbook. Teachers' plan books provide evidence of this, as do principals' observations of the manner in which teachers are spending instructional time.

An important observation about teacher behavior concerns the amount of time that teachers are spending with questioning and student participation in learning activities in the classroom — as opposed to lecture and seat work. Video-taping of teaching practice is a common event, with the principal and the teacher reviewing the tape. These tapes, as well as daily drop-in visits by the principal, clearly document positive changes in teacher performance.

According to the teachers, two things kept them from using new techniques in the classroom: they needed help to use the technique properly, and they feared the new techniques would quickly be replaced by others.

An important aspect of the staff development program is peer observation. All teachers observe one of their peers each year and conference with that teacher concerning what they see. The results of these observations are private. Administrators assist only in arranging visit and conference times.

To build commitment for staff development activity, planning begins well in advance and involves the people who will be directly affected. In 1987-88, the school district began a three-year initiative in curriculum development. Initial planning was done through the superintendent's advisory committee, made up of several teachers from each building. Teachers presented grade level, curriculum, and staff development concerns. Once the general focus was agreed upon, members from the advisory group, other key teachers, and administrators in the various buildings visited other sites with similar developments underway. From these visits and earlier discussions, the committee put together a survey document that offered a broad group of people the opportunity to respond to different possible options. All the data were compiled, and a course of action was chosen.

Harrison found that an important outgrowth of the staff development program was that teachers voluntarily interacted with principals to ask for suggestions and to give advice on the school program. He stated in a recent letter:

> Teachers are asking for staff development activities above and beyond the "official" activities. They are not saying "Let's add another staff development day to the calendar," but they are saying the following:
>
>> We need to find ways to extend these basic objectives beyond rote skills. When can we have some time to talk about that?
>>
>> We need some ideas for working with those students who finish their work ahead of everyone else. They have too much unproductive time. Can you give us some assistance with that?
>
> In other words, teachers are becoming more aware, through staff development activities, that there are solutions to problems, that other teachers and districts have experienced the same kinds of problems that they themselves experience, and that a variety of strategies exist that can be successfully brought to bear on almost any problem.
>
> Another unplanned effect is that follow-up activities are not always what we had originally planned for them to be. For example, as teachers realize how many of the state's basic skills are written at the knowledge and comprehension levels, they want to investigate ways to insure that those skills will move to at least the application level in their own teaching of the skills. At their request, our staff development meetings will combine the K-7 faculty to review Bloom's Taxonomy and how it needs to be approached in our basic curriculum. This was not anticipated last April when we reviewed needs assessments, but if good teaching in the classroom means that we must monitor learners' progress and adjust our teaching accordingly, then good staff development dictates that we do the same thing.[57]

Pontotoc schools set upon a course to redesign how students and teachers interact in the classroom. With virtually no increase in the budget for the activities a substantial change in the quality of the program occurred.

SPRINGDALE

Location:	Northwest Arkansas
Type of District:	Small city/rural
Population:	23,458
Student Enrollment:	7,366
Racial Mix:	99.5% white
Per Pupil Expenditure:	$2,400
Students Receiving Free & Reduced-Price Lunch:	20%
Reform Area:	Redesigning the schools

Springdale is a small city located in northwest Arkansas immediately north of Fayetteville, home of the University of Arkansas. The last report of student enrollment was 7,366. There are eight elementary schools (K-6), two junior high schools (7-9), and one high school (10-12) with 1,700 students.

Superintendent Jim Rollins described the 1986-87 school year as a watershed year for Springdale. The district gained compliance with the new and tough State of Arkansas Education Standards, Governor Bill Clinton chose the district as one of two school districts in the state to represent Arkansas in the National Governor's study of 16 school districts in the "Time for Results" report, and Ted Sizer tapped the school district to participate in the Coalition of Essential Schools project. This year also marked the second year since John Goodlad had selected the school district to become a member of the Arkansas Educational Renewal Consortium (AERC).

The National Governor's Association Task Force asked the school district to focus on three major areas of interest:

- developing an experimental program which, through redesigning the organization of the high school, creates a more productive working/learning environment;

- developing a structure and climate which allows for effective parental involvement in partnership with the school district; and

- establishing an alternative program that increases the holding power of the high school.

The Springdale High School-Within-a-School (SWS) project was in its third year in 1988-89. It involved four teachers — Fran Flynt, Melinda Nickel, Steve Poynter, and Jim Rees — and 55 students, 3% of the high school student body. Apparently, original plans as described by Principal John Delap were to expand the program over three years by the formula: first year — 4 teachers, 80 students; second year — 8 teachers, 160 students; and third year — 12 teachers, 240 students. Delap resigned in mid-year of the first project year. The expansion did not occur.

In 1988, the SWS day consisted of four instructional hours in which students were taught four courses: Inquiry and Expression, History and Philosophy, Science and Mathematics, and Literature and the Arts. The remainder of the day was spent taking courses from the regular high school curriculum.

The other project with national connections is the Goodlad project, as represented by the Arkansas Educational Renewal Consortium (AERC). Nine other school districts and two Arkansas universities (Arkansas and Central Arkansas) comprise the state group. AERC was funded by a grant from the Winthrop Rockefeller Foundation. The intent of the Goodlad project "is to maintain, justify and articulate sound, comprehensive programs of instruction for children and youth." Through 1988 Rollins was on the executive AERC board. Other coalition representatives in the school district were Nancy Roark, Administrative principal at SHS; Sandra Posey, an elementary teacher; and Sandy Fanning, a junior high math teacher, who saw the project as "primarily trying to improve communication within districts."

Springdale is a sound, well-administered public school district in its own right. Through October 1988, I could find little direct effect that participation in the Goodlad project had on the district. The district had independently implemented a number of activities that would meet the Goodlad guidelines but could not be traced to consortium activity. I judged the district ahead of developments that might result from AERC activity.

The School-Within-a-School Project (SWS) is operating successfully within narrow bounds. Educationally it does accomplish what Sizer hoped would occur. The method of instructing students is quite different from regular high school instruction. It is successful. It has inconsequential influence on the school district beyond its four dedicated teachers and 55 students.

There seems to be little hope that the project will continue beyond the life of the foundation support. The project imposes many strains on the people in the Springdale High School culture. This is to be expected. There was, and has been, limited effort to prepare the total school community for its presence or to integrate SWS as a modifier of the regular program. The project burst upon an "unsuspecting SHS faculty" (in the words of one person interviewed) through print and video publicity. Many faculty members resented the fact that in the first project year they, the majority, were referred to as out-worlders. Other teachers resent small class loads and the differential in planning time in the project teachers' schedule. Despite excellent training given the project staff, the early loss of the principal who started the program took away some of the support that might otherwise have been expected. Negative notes were heard from the SWS faculty. As one said, "What I did not bargain for was the emotional investment that I had to make in this program." As a whole I found no renorming outside of the project to support the SWS program over the long term.

The Springdale district is a sound school district. It has many positive factors working to strengthen the school program over time. The superintendent's cabinet has several "shelf groups" that meet once a month to advise the district administrators — for example, a Patron's Shelf, representing 35 recognized leadership groups in the community, who are parents as well as organizational members; and a Certified Shelf, 15 representatives from each school building. All are considered as stakeholders in advising the leadership of the school district.

There is a consistent assessment of student achievement based on the idea that achievement tests should assess what is actually taught in the school district. Curriculum guides, instructional activity, and assessment efforts are coordinated. Specific instructional goals are set as general guidelines for instruction.

There is an "early prevention of failure" program operating in grades 4, 5, and 6, where a professional team screens each child and prepares developmental activities for each. In addition, the district has implemented the following programs: kindergarten screening and alternative instructional activities for kindergartners are major efforts; improving writing and language arts skills; an alternative school for high-risk students, independent of the SWS; a model cooperative education program for elementary students, operated in cooperation with the University of Arkansas; and a model Developmental Economics Education Program.

The faculty, staff, and central office personnel interviewed were uniformly positive about the overall direction of the school district. The Springdale school district appears to be well above average in most aspects for a small city school district. It does not appear to be undergoing any substantial restructuring, though the quality of its school program does appear to be in robust health and strengthening.

ARDMORE

Location:	Southcentral Oklahoma
Type of District:	Small city/rural
Population:	25,000
Student Enrollment:	3,300
Racial Mix:	66% white, 22% African American, 10% Indian, 2% other
Per Pupil Expenditure:	$3,050
Students Receiving Free & Reduced-Price Lunch:	51%
Reform Area:	Restructuring mathematics and language arts

The Ardmore school district is located in the heart of the Oklahoma Territory originally assigned to the Chickasaw Nation. Ardmore schools serve students who reside within the city limits and some of the territory in Carter County. Approximately 3,300 students attend programs on ten campuses. The district includes one kindergarten center, six elementary schools (1-5), one sixth grade center, one middle school (7-8), and Ardmore High School.

Ardmore is a school district that has attempted a major restructuring of the teaching of language arts and mathematics in grades K-8. The purpose of the program as defined by Superintendent Howard Thomas is to "move on the ones who can and assist those who are frustrated."

The project began in the summer of 1985 under the leadership of then superintendent Weldon Perrin. Its goals as outlined by the project director at the time, Deanne Broughton, were to implement the following recommendations of the Sid W. Richardson Foundation Study of exemplary programs for high-ability youth:

- broaden the process for assessing ability;

- adopt a school program that uses continuous progress and appropriate pacing;

- use many different options to promote student learning; and

- seek cooperation with many different community agencies with a stake in assisting learners of differing ability.

Other features of the program included Advanced Placement, the International Baccalaureate, mentoring, internships, and concurrent enrollments in institutions of higher learning.

The Richardson study examined a number of exemplary programs for high-ability students around the nation. It found that most programs were fragmented — that few districts attempt a comprehensive K-12 plan for all able learners. In 1985, the Ardmore school district, with limited financial assistance from the Kerr and Noble Foundations, implemented a model which would solve this problem. Their program would advance students at whatever pace was most natural for them and provide the most challenge. This was to be done in all 10 schools and at all grade levels. The total cost of the three-year project was to be $89,000 annually for a total of $269,000 for the effort. The two foundations and the district were to share the cost equally. In addition, there was to be cooperative effort with area colleges.

To broaden student assessment, the district accepted no single determiner of intelligence, used a wider range of testing strategies, and avoided labels and arbitrary cutoffs. The adoption of continuous progress allowed students to move ahead as they mastered content and skills, and allowed students to enroll at more than one grade level if abilities varied widely in different subject matter. Programming options were comprehensive — across disciplines, grade levels, and differing levels of ability. Programs were carefully articulated across grade levels and throughout the system. The community was to be an active partner in providing services.

Project development activities include:

- conducting needs assessment for planning staff development;

- developing record-keeping procedures to facilitate assessment, placement, instruction, pacing and evaluation;

- assessing student abilities and degree of previous learning to determine present level of performance and implications for pacing;

- providing administrative arrangements to accommodate instructional groups with similar needs;

- developing curricular materials beginning with lower grade levels;

- conducting staff development activities; developing the concept of shared staff accountability for students and program success through team planning;

- utilizing a campus team of volunteers composed of principal, staff, parents, and students (at secondary levels) to interpret and build support for the program;

- utilizing a community team of volunteers composed of business, industry, university, and advocacy groups to provide resources (primary and secondary sources) to program;

- collecting and storing student data for assessment, diagnosis, and evaluation purposes; and

- publishing progress reports documenting accomplishment of both process and product objectives at end of year two and three.

In the fall of 1988, the Ardmore pyramid project is struggling, but alive. Many of the bright hopes of the project were considerably dimmed by financial hard times. The school district budget suffered severe cuts when Oklahoma contributions decreased due to the collapse of the oil market in the "oil patch."

Project director Broughton was a staff cutback. The academically demanding International Diploma at the high school was also terminated in staff cutbacks. Despite this, the continuous progress phase of the program has been continued in K-8 language arts and mathematics. The broadened interpretation of *gifted* has been incorporated as designed. A strengthened curriculum has resulted in higher achievement scores.

Analysis of the planning and implementation steps shows that initial planning was primarily a top-down activity. There were opportunities for community and teacher input into the planning process. There were expectations that the process was linear and orderly. By the summer of 1986, however, the faculty was fully aware that the new procedures were difficult to put in place and manage in operation. A number of teacher voices were raised beginning in the summer of 1986 asking that the project be dropped. By the summer of 1987, faculty voices had been joined by some from the community asking that the program be abandoned. A thorough review of the program in the 1987-88 school year showed conclusively that the program was an academic success. By the fall of 1987, renorming apparently began to take place within the school community. The comment was frequently heard that though the process was troublesome the results in student learning were well worth the effort.

The assessment of the Ardmore redesign effort is that it represented a major effort to change the way students were taught. Despite unexpected financial problems, loss of the project director, and the job change of the superintendent, the central office staff, along with the the principal, and some teacher advocates enabled the work to move forward with a substantial degree of success.

SOCIAL CIRCLE

Location:	Northcentral Georgia
Type of District:	Small city/rural
Population:	2,591
Student Enrollment:	1,000
Racial Mix:	60% white, 40% African American
Per Pupil Expenditure:	$2,733
Students Receiving Free & Reduced-Price Lunch	38%
Reform Area:	Mastery learning

The Social Circle school district strives for academic excellence, providing an educational program that ensures the best possible future for each of its 1,000 students. Social Circle's population is 2,591. Its claim to fame is that it was burned by General Sherman in 1864 after the battle at nearby Atlanta. The system consists of three schools — Social Circle Elementary (K-5), Social Circle Middle School (6-8) and Social Circle High School (9-12). Ten years ago there would have been no dispute in the community in consolidating its 40% minority student body with the virtually 100% caucasian population in Marion County. Today the school community vigorously resists any such initiative. Local officials say the Social Circle schools are too strong academically to abandon.

The Social Circle school district has been undergoing substantial change since 1976, when John Burks became superintendent. In the late 1970s the district became one of the districts studied by John Goodlad in his *Study of Schooling*.

In a recent statement Burks explained why he took drastic measures to change the school program:

> Born from a need to improve, Social Circle had test scores in the lower 25% of all systems in Georgia on the Criterion-referenced test (CRT) and the Iowa Test of Basic Skills. Faced with an intervention from certain parents in our federal court order asserting that their children did not have the same educational opportunity in Social Circle as they would have in the Walton County System [Social Circle straddles a county line], I embraced the philosophy and began to look at implementation [of mastery learning].
>
> I visited Johnson City [New York], and saw a positive successful instructional program built around mastery learning (ML) philosophy and outcome-based (OB) grade and course objectives.
>
> We adopted ML philosophy and decided upon a course of implementation in 1980. The model selected for implementation had to have three major components:

I. Use of existing data to establish need for change:
    A. test scores
    B. court order
    C. private school enrollment
    D. school climate
    E. school suspension discipline problems

II. Method of introducing research and successful implementation:
    A. articles on successes and nature of program
    B. staff development
    C. visit to Johnson City by people critical to implementation
    D. establishing system by which regular discussion could occur between all parties — principal, teachers, parents, etc. This gave birth to grade level teams — the introductory meetings in homes and churches; rewriting of curriculum so as to reflect OB goals

III. Evaluation:
    A. Testing program to evaluate academic progress (our charts for grade level progress cover five years)
    B. team meeting model
    C. our regular staff meetings

This implementation also had a community component — school-established and school-operated youth recreation programs. This placed the school in a positive relationship with parents. I was the director and used coaches (school employees) to operate little league baseball, football, and basketball. We expanded this to include computer camp and summer camping.

The [school] board had originally requested only promotion standards, which under the circumstances would have been punitive. With ML, summer school became a support and second chance to master grade-level objectives for promotion.[58]

Staff development was one key to implementation of a mastery learning (ML) program in Social Circle City Schools. Mastery learning is based on the philosophy of Benjamin Bloom that almost all students can master those concepts and skills considered important enough to be taught in school. This occurs if they are given appropriate instruction and sufficient time to learn. Mastery learning offers an approach to outcome-based education that is systematic yet humanistic.

In 1979 Burks initiated a weekly staff development session for 28 elementary school teachers during the 3:10-4:00 p.m. planning time that is part of the working schedule in the system. Teachers began revising curriculum to reflect the objectives-based approach.

Teachers made it clear from the start that they wanted to pay attention to the social and academic needs of students. The Social Circle program focused on the "whole student" in the manner of Dewey's participatory model development of both self-reliance and social cooperation, yet also addressed academic skills and concepts to ensure achievement.

Guides in the development of the Social Circle ML program were the school system of Johnson City, New York, and the writings of Benjamin Bloom, James R. Block, Lorin Anderson, and John Champlin.[59]

With the new ML model, instruction became teacher-paced or directed. Teachers first reviewed all prerequisite skills with the class as a whole to motivate them and used various motivational techniques, and then exposed all children to the identified objective, using instructional techniques of their own choosing.

After the students in each ML group were exposed to an objective through directed teaching activities, they were given opportunities to practice the new concept or skill with the careful monitoring of the teacher. Each teacher was asked to model the behavior expected of students when they mastered the objective. When students were able to proceed on their own, there were opportunities for independent practice or peer study while the teacher worked with other groups of children in the classroom and homework assignments.

After independent practice, teachers administered a "formative" test, which was not graded but used for diagnostic purposes. After this test was given and the children's responses analyzed, the children were placed in subgroups for "correctives" or "extensions." Correctives involve reteaching of those aspects of the objective not yet mastered, and extensions were activities designed to develop higher levels of skills and understandings. Children in correctives groups were exposed to different instructional approaches in the reteaching sessions.

Children who did not master the objective at the agreed upon proficiency level were carried forward with the rest of their group to the next objective. But they were also placed in newly formed groups of children from other classrooms who were experiencing difficulty with the same objective for further instruction by a teacher freed by his/her mastery team for this purpose, by compensatory program teachers, by special education personnel, and even by community volunteers.

Special characteristics of the program have been

- identifying and stating behaviorally the grade-level instructional objectives;

- setting promotion standards for each grade level which embody the most essential ML objectives;

- writing and rewriting of curriculum guides and instructional materials to correspond to the instructional process model adopted for the system;

- selecting and adapting textbooks and other teacher materials to fit the adopted ML instructional process model;

- organizing multi-graded and within-grade teams of children and teachers to facilitate flexible scheduling of children for continuous progress;

- developing a system for monitoring student progress and for documentation of promotion standards;

- developing an awareness of different student learning styles and varied ways of addressing them;

- organizing team meetings so that they are productive and yet still focused on personal growth and development of both team members and children;

- developing a classroom and school climate which contributes to positive student self-concepts;

- establishing a common language for talking about instructional and administrative concerns;

- learning how and when to share decision-making responsibilities with the principal and central office staff;

- coordinating support services and programs (special education, compensatory programs and personnel) so that ML objectives are reinforced at all times;

- utilizing all school personnel, including the librarian, principal, and teaching aides fully in the instruction of ML objectives;

- communicating to parents and the community at large the advantages to their children of the ML program;

- managing teacher-parent conferences so that parents are helped to be cooperative partners with their children's teachers;

- training and scheduling community volunteers to work directly with children and teachers in classrooms; and

- fostering a continuing sense of community within the school through continuing discussion of the mastery learning concept and its theoretical assumptions.

The mastery learning project has been underway in Social Circle for eight years. It is a stable and accepted part of the operating program of the school district. Staff development and maintenance activity is constant. Old skills are constantly reinforced; new staff members are carefully indoctrinated into the program. Staff members have a positive self-image and understand the procedures necessary to make the program operate successfully. Developmental costs for the program have been minimal.

Academic results have been excellent. Despite the fact that nearly half the student body are eligible for free and reduced-price lunches, achievement test scores for the district are above national averages and above the average for the state of Georgia.

RICHMOND COUNTY

Location	Eastcentral Georgia
Type of District	Small city/rural
Population	181,629
Student Enrollment	33,000
Racial Mix	Predominantly African American
Per Pupil Expenditure	$2,900
Students Receiving Free & Reduced-Price Lunch	75%
Reform Area	Staff development

Augusta, Georgia, is the home of the Masters Golf Tournament. It is also the second largest metropolitan area in Georgia, with a population of over 400,000. The Richmond County school district serves Augusta and the Richmond County. The student population is predominantly African American and low income. There are 9 high schools, 8 middle schools, and 33 elementary schools.

The Richmond County School Improvement Program represents an effort by a school district to change the "workplace of teaching and improve the achievements of students and their aptitude to learn"[60]

In the winter of 1987, Superintendent John Strelec assigned Dr. Carlene Murphy, Director of Staff Development, to outline the development project. She did so, using the Models of Teaching ideas of education consultants Bruce Joyce and Beverly Showers. From that time until the contract was signed, over 19 meetings were held in the school district. Many different people were involved in determining that this model of schooling was a desirable route for the district to follow. The following spring the school board contracted with Joyce and Showers to oversee and coordinate activities of this remarkable project.

This special school program was initiated because a combination of widely divergent new programs and staff development initiatives previously used had not improved student achievement to the extent hoped. Many thought that a radical change of direction in the nature of the school program was needed.

In March of 1987, the state of Georgia appropriated nearly $23 million dollars to compensate teachers for participating in summer training. Richmond County Schools' share of this for summer stipends was $600,000. These funds made possible the chance to bring about gains in student achievement by implementing a program that would involve a massive retraining of the school staff.

The philosophy grew in the school district to use many community resources to improve the quality of student learning. The state of Georgia mandated intense testing and data evaluation, as well as curriculum planning and development.

Development initiatives, as described by Murphy and her colleagues, were

— to generate student growth by having teachers in a few schools learn to use teaching strategies to increase student ability to work cooperatively, memorize material, and generate conceptual thinking;

— to strive toward substantial increases in student learning — a goal of 0.5 standard deviation or about 17 percentile points on standard tests of achievement for each of two years; and

— to prepare a cadre of teachers who could, in the future, expand the program by offering service to other teachers and administrators.

The first year's effort would be concentrated on several "target" schools and the initial preparation of the cadre. The second year, efforts would continue to support the target schools, begin the operation of the cadre in other sites, and prepare additional cadre members.[61]

The decision had been made to change the way the professionals in the school district thought about teaching by adopting four teaching models as supplements to any techniques that teachers were already using:

Assists to Memory — teaching children how to use mnemonic devices and associational procedures which increase memory;

Concept Attainment — teaching children to focus their cognitive skills, to form hypotheses, to examine information, and to apply concepts;

Cooperative Learning — in conjunction with the other models, teaching children to manage social energy and to improve achievement through collaborative learning experiences;

Inductive Thinking — teaching children how to collect and categorize data, to form concepts, to interpret data, and to apply concepts.

The district central office planners saw that the implementation of training would have a substantial impact on the relationships among teachers and principals as well as curriculum and instruction and general school improvement. In February 1987 Superintendent John Strelec shared the staff development plans with his board, central office staff, and the directors of curriculum, testing, and the Chapter One programs. After much discussion the decision was made to put the plans into operation.

The plan that evolved linked four related innovations: all teachers in the target schools would be organized in study groups; building administrators and study teams leaders would examine the learning climate of the schools to choose areas for improvement; the faculties would receive training in models of teaching designed to improve aspects of student learning; and a group of trained teachers and administrators would offer training to other teachers and administrators.

Joyce and Showers used the following process:

> Principals were invited to a meeting, the project was explained, and they were given readings about the models of teaching. Joyce taught an inductive lesson to a group of middle school students to begin to orient himself and Showers to the children. There was a dialogue about the rationale and the practical questions of implementation. Joyce pointed out the need for balance in grouping for appropriate instruction and avoiding isolation of the lowest-achieving students. Joyce maintained that models of teaching are not learning-style specific and that students who have difficulty responding to a particular model may be the very ones who need them most. A meeting with the evaluation staff centered on procedures for measuring student achievement. A tentative plan was worked out that would involve matching each student in the target schools with students in other instructional settings.[62]

In time principals and teachers were invited to express interest in participating in the project. A number responded positively. The three with the highest level of commitment to the expectations were the East Augusta Middle School, Barton Chapel Elementary, and Wheeless Road Elementary. (Three of 50 is a tiny fraction of district schools — the task to be completed is a massive undertaking.) Murphy stated that all the returning faculty of each participating school had indicated a full commitment:

- to attend all training sessions during the summer and complete all assignments;

- to prepare and do demonstration teaching during the intensive two weeks of training and to practice with peers regularly throughout the summer;

- to employ the new teaching strategies introduced during the training on a daily basis throughout the year;

- to work with peer study groups during the year, planning lessons and visiting one another in the classroom;

- to participate in regular training activities during the school year;

- to make videotapes of their teaching on a regular basis; and

- to participate in a similar program in the summer of 1988 and during the 1988-89 school year.[63]

In May 1987, 104 teachers from the target schools were enrolled to take the summer training. By June 1 the number of meetings to prepare for the initiative had reached 43. Documentation of the summer and fall activities from project leaders Carlene Murphy, Joe Murphy, Bruce Joyce, and Beverly Showers report the following activity:

> The initial phase focused on exposing participants to several teaching strategies.
>
> The summer would begin with one week of intensive training, followed by six weeks of practice and design of lessons for the fall, followed by another intensive week of training. All participants were asked to practice each of the teaching strategies in September and October no less than thirty times apiece and to strive to have the teaching strategies mastered as part of their active repertoire by the end of October. The peer coaching teams would meet weekly and, between meetings, visit one another in the classroom and study the children's responses to the teaching strategies.
>
> For nearly all members of the group, there was great anxiety at the beginning of the summer training. One was simply the seriousness of the district's intent that the content be actually implemented as the school year began.
>
> From the very first demonstrations, many of the participants manifested the belief that their students were not capable of using the models. The models involved teaching students to study together, and many teachers turned out to believe that cooperative study was beyond their students' grasps. Similarly many did not believe their students could think conceptually, either to attain or form categories, or that they could learn strategies for memorizing material. The trainers were adamant that the students could learn the necessary skills and that it was important for the teachers to elevate their expectations about what the students could do. This conflict was a major test of the innovation — could the teachers come to embrace the idea that the students could learn to be more powerful learners?
>
> The teaching models conflicted with many of the trainees' beliefs about teaching and learning. Many felt that cooperative study was inherently more inefficient than individual study. Many felt that conceptual learning would be inefficient even if it were possible. Mnemonic devices were viewed with suspicion by quite a percentage of the participants.
>
> Mnemonic devices were employed to teach them the names and locations of various countries and they practiced by teaching one another similar content. They analyzed the language of Tom Wolfe and James Mitchener. They wrote reactions to film clips and classified their own language uses. They observed tapes of demonstration lessons with children. They had to confront the state of their own language skills and the implications for their teaching. For some, writing, sharing, and analyzing their work was extremely uncomfortable.

Although many of the teachers succeeded in practicing their new models until the students became able to respond effectively, and although the study groups met regularly, observing one another was very anxiety-producing for most, and peer-coaching interaction was not very well implemented.

In all three schools the struggle to plan lessons generated discussion about what concepts and information were most important in the curriculum. The schools generated increasing amounts of collective activity.

It was first in the middle school that a faculty as a whole began to be concretely aware that their labors were bearing fruit as disciplinary referrals for the more serious breaches of discipline dropped by fifty percent below the level of the previous year. Most attributed the drop to the greater cohesiveness and sense of mission in the faculty, the use of the highly involving teaching strategies, and the impact of the cooperative study on other aspects of the students' social behavior. Also, the teachers who were using new repertoire more actively began to report that the students were, in fact, able to develop the skills to learn from them.[64]

Results in the spring and fall of 1988 show that the project is being well received. Interviews with randomly selected teachers and principals involved in the project indicate that the teaching skills are difficult to learn, but they feel are well worth the trouble in improved student attitude and academic performance.

Charlotte R. Sudderth, assistant principal at East Augusta Middle School is enthusiastic about the developments:

The interdisciplinary study groups of six is a good idea. We are not given a package to study. We treat each other as learners. It is difficult to work this way because we are not used to being together all day learning and applying new skills.

We do it on our own — they do provide ideas to match your plan. This provides us with the ownership of the ideas we develop.

Georgia's Outcome-Based Education program fits right in to the components of the program. I see it making us stronger in delivery of student skills.

We are definitely in a period of adjustment. Teachers are learning many new strategies. The four procedures add alternatives to seatwork and lecture because what we do causes more student participation and teaches children how to take responsibility for their own learning — thinking logically, taking data, observing — teaching kids how to use the abilities they have.[65]

Richmond County schools has a start on renorming a school society. Several years will be necessary to determine if it can involve the entire school district. The high schools will be the acid test of this program's success.

NOTES

[1]Deal, Terry E. and A. A. Kennedy. *Corporate Cultures: The Rites and Rituals of Corporate Life*. Reading, Mass.: Addison-Wesley Publishing, 1982.

[2]"The Culture of An Effective School." Research Action Brief Number 22. ERIC Clearinghouse on Educational Management, National Institute of Education. (ERIC Document Reproduction Service ED 252 912.) p. 2, February 1984.

[3]Schmuck, Richard A. *Organizational Development in Schools: Contemporary Conceptual Practices*. Eugene, Ore.: Center on Organizational Development in Schools (ERIC Document Reproduction Service ED 278 119). 1987.

[4]March, James G. "The Technology of Foolishness." In James G. March and Johan P. Olsen (eds.), *Ambiguity and Choice in Organizations*. Bergen, Norway: Universitetsforlaget, 1976.

[5]Joyce, Bruce and Beverly Showers. "Improving Teacher Training: The Message of Research." *Educational Leadership*. vol. 37, no. 5, 1980, pp. 379-85.

[6]Fullan, Michael, Matthew Miles, and Gib Taylor. *OD in Schools: The State of the Art*. (5 vols.) Toronto: Ontario Institute for the Study of Education, 1978.

[7]Schmuck, Richard and Philip J. Runkel. "Theory and Technology of Organizational Development." In Mary F. Callan and Frances M. Trusty (eds.), *Organizational Development*. Bloomington, Ind.: Phi Delta Kappa, 1987, p. 7.

[8]Roark, Albert E. and Wallace E. Davis, Jr. "Staff Development and Organizational Development." In Betty Dillon-Peterson (ed.), *ASCD Yearbook*. Arlington, Va.: Association for Supervision and Curriculum Development, 1981, pp. 37-57.

[9]Goodlad, John I. "Toward a Healthy Ecosystem: The Ecology of School Renewal." In John I. Goodlad (ed.), *Eighty-sixth Yearbook of the National Society of the Study of Education*, Chicago: University of Chicago Press, 1987, pp. 210-21.

[10]For insights into the history and the concept of general systems theory see:

Klir, George J. *Architecture of Systems Problem Solving*. New York: Plenum Press, 1985. (A mathematical model of systems theory for the serious minded.)

Pugh, D.S. (ed.) *Systems Thinking: Selected Readings*. Baltimore: Penguin Books. 1969. (Very readable nontechnical explanation of open and closed systems and their operation as human systems.)

Wiener, Norbert. "Cybernetics." In S. Ulmer (ed.), *Introductory Readings in Political Science*, Chicago, Ill.: Rand McNally, 1961, pp. 298-306. (Nontechnical.)

Wiener, Norbert. *The Human Use of Human Beings*. Boston: Houghton Mifflin, 1950. (A nontechnical history of the development of the concept.)

[11]Immegart, Glenn L. and Francis J. Pilecki. *An Introduction to Systems Analysis for the Educational Administrator*. Reading, Mass.: Addison-Wesley Publishing, 1973.

[12]Ibid., pp. 34.

[13]Ibid., pp. 34-35.

[14]Schmuck and Runkel, 1985, p. 6.

[15]Immegart and Pilecki, 1973, pp. 35.

[16]Ibid., 1973, pp. 36.

[17]Ibid., 1973, pp. 37.

[18]Filbeck, Robert. *Systems in Teaching and Learning*. Lincoln, Neb.: Professional Educators Publications, 1974, pp. 19-20.

[19]Schmuck and Runkel, 1985, p. 6.

[20]Immegart and Pilecki, 1973, p. 38.

[21]Ibid., pp. 39.

[22]Ibid., pp. 41.

[23]Ibid., pp. 41.

[24]Goodlad, 1987, p. 210.

[25]Ibid., p. 213.

[26]Immegart and Pilecki, 1973, p. 41.

[27]Schmuck and Runkel, 1985, p. 8.

[28]In systems theory this is known as the concept of equifinality, or to quote an ancient proverb, all roads lead to Rome. Immegart and Pilecki, 1973, p. 42.

[29]Ibid., p. 42.

[30]Personal conversation with John Burks, February 1988.

[31]Schmuck and Runkel, 1985, p. 14.

[32]Immegart and Pilecki, 1973, p. 43.

[33]Liebermann, Ann and Lynne Miller. "School Improvement: Themes and Variations." *Teachers College Record*, vol. 86, no. 1 (Fall 1984), p. 7.

[34]Immegart and Pilecki, 1973, p. 44.

[35]Ibid., p. 45.

[36]Raporport, A. "Mathematical Aspects of General Systems Analysis." *General Systems*, vol. 11, 1966, p. 3.

[37]Ekholm, Mats, et al. "Studies of the Innovation Process in Compulsory Schools." Stockholm: National Swedish Board of Education. *School Research Newsletter*. (ERIC Document Reproduction Service ED 279 090), November 1986, p. 7.

[38]Peters, Tom and Nancy Austin. *A Passion for Excellence*. New York: Random House, 1985, p. 284.

[39]Joyce, Bruce. Comments made to the steering committee of the Models of Teaching Program, Richmond County Public Schools, Augusta, Georgia, January 26, 1988.

[40]Chubb, John E. "Why the Current Wave of School Reform Will Fail." *The Public Interest*, vol. 90 (Winter 1988), p. 39.

[41]Ibid., p. 38.

[42]See, for example: Goodlad, 1987; Chubb, 1988; Firestone, William, A. and Bruce L. Wilson, *Using Bureaucratic and Cultural Linkages to Improve Instruction: The High School Principal's Contribution*. Philadelphia, Pa.: Field Studies Component, Research and Evaluation Division, Research for Better Schools, Inc. (November 1983).

[43]Firestone and Wilson, 1983, p. 12-14.

[44]Prince, Julian. "Effective Roles for Middle Managers in Outcome-Based Schools. *Outcomes*, vol. 3, no. 1, Summer/Fall 1983, pp. 10-20.
_____. "Formative Teacher Evaluation: The Crucial Element in all Outcome-Based Education Programs." In Karen Kline (ed.), *Evaluation of Teaching: The Formative Process*. Bloomington, Ind.: Phi Delta Kappa Center on Evaluation, Development, and Research Hot Topics series, 1984, pp. 85-94.
_____. "Preparing Principals as Instructional Leaders in Effective Schools: A Successful Plan of Action. *Spectrum*, vol. 2, no. 2 (Spring 1984), pp. 3-10.

[45]Firestone and Wilson, 1983, pp. 14-16.

[46]Jacullo-Noto, Joann. "Teachers: Behavioral Characteristics of Emerging Leaders." Paper presented to the American Association of Colleges of Teacher Education. New Orleans, Louisiana, February 1988, p. 12.

[47]Goodlad, John I. "Understanding Schools is Basic to Improving Them." *National Forum of Applied Educational Research Journal*, vol. 1, no. 2, 1987, pp. 1-9. (See pages 4 and 5.)

[48]Patterson, Jerry L., Stewart C. Purkey, and Jackson V. Parker. *Productive School Systems for a Nonrational World*. Alexandria, Va.: Association for Supervision and Curriculum Development, 1986.

[49]Patterson, Purkey, Parker, p. 32.

[50]Ibid., p. 33.

[51]Karrass, Chester L. "Winning in Negotiations." *Government Executive*, vol. 9, no. 9 (September 1977), p. 36.

[52]Prince, Julian D. "Implementing Desegregation: McComb, Mississippi." In Eugene C. Lee (ed.), *School Desegregation: Retrospect and Prospect*. Atlanta: Southern Newspaper Publishers Association, Foundation Seminar Books, 1970, p. 130.

[53]Minutes of the Tupelo, Mississippi school board meeting, 1976.

[54]Tyler, Ralph W. "Education Reforms." *Phi Delta Kappan*, vol. 69, no. 4 (December 1987), p. 280.

[55]Rice, Eugene and Ann Austin. "High Faculty Morale." *Change*, vol. 20 (March/April 1988), pp. 50-58.

[56]Harrison recommends the following readings:

English, Fenwick W. *Curriculum Management for Schools, Colleges, and Business.* Springfield, Ill.: Charles C. Thomas Publisher, 1987.

Evertson, Carolyn and Edmund T. Emmer, Barbara S. Clements, Julie P. Sanford and Murray E. Worsham. *Classroom Management for Elementary Teachers*. Englewood Cliffs, N.J.: Prentice-Hall, 1984.

Hunter, Madeline. *Mastery Teaching*. El Segundo, Calif.: TIP Publications, 1982.

Hunter, Madeline and George Barker. "If At First . . .: Attribution Theory in the Classroom." *Educational Leadership*. vol. 45, no. 2 (October 1987) pp. 50-53.

[57]Personal correspondence with Charles Harrison March 23, 1988.

[58]Personal correspondence with John Burks March 1, 1988.

[59]These are the readings that Burks suggested:

Anderson, Loren. "Instruction and Time-on-Task: A Review." *Journal of Curriculum Studies*, vol. 13, no. 4, 1981, pp. 289-303.

Block, J.H. (ed.) *Schools, Society and Mastery Learning*. New York: Holt, Rinehart and Winston, 1974.

Block, J.H. (ed.) *Mastery Learning: Theory and Practice*. New York: Holt, Rinehart & Winston, 1971.

Bloom, Benjamin S. and L.A. Sosniak. "Talent Development vs. Schooling." *Educational Leadership*, vol. 89, no. 2 (November 1981), pp. 86-94.

Bloom, Benjamin S. *Human Characteristics and School Learning*. New York: McGraw-Hill, 1976.

Champlin, John R. "Is Creating an Outcome-Based Program Worth the Effort? A Superintendent's Perspective." A mimeographed paper (1981) available from the author.

Champlin, John R. "A Student's Second Chance." *NYSSEA Journal*, October 1980, pp. 16-18.

Dewey, John. *The Child and The Curriculum*. New York: Teachers College Press, 1950 (originally published 1902).

[60]Murphy, Carlene U., Joseph A. Murphy, Bruce Joyce, and Beverly Showers (January 20, 1988). "The Richmond County School Improvement Program: Preparation and Initial Phase." An article submitted to the *Journal of Staff Development*. Augusta, Ga.: Richmond County Public Schools, January 20, 1988, p. 1. Permission to quote from Carlene U. Murphy. For updates on program developments contact Carlene U. Murphy, Director of Staff Development, The William Robinson Staff Development Center, 804 Katharine Street, Augusta, Georgia 30904.

[61]Murphy, Murphy, Joyce and Showers, 1988, p. 9.

[62]Ibid., p. 12-13.

[63]Ibid., p. 14-15.

[64]Ibid., p. 17-19.

[65]Private conversation with Charlotte R. Sudderth.